The Permanent Pleasure

The answer is, that nothing can permanently please, which does not contain in itself the reason why it is so, and not otherwise.

—Coleridge, *Biographia Literaria*, Chapter 14.

The Permanent Pleasure
Essays on Classics of Romanticism

RICHARD HARTER FOGLE

University of Georgia Press, Athens

Library of Congress Catalog Card Number: 72–86784
International Standard Book Number: 0-8203-0311-9

The University of Georgia Press, Athens 30602

Special Acknowledgments

The author and the publisher are indebted to the following journals, organizations, and institutions for permission to reprint these essays: to the *Bucknell Review* for "Dante and Shelley's *Adonais*," *Bucknell Review*, 15 (1967), 11–21; to the *D. H. Lawrence Review* for "Beauty and Truth: J. M. Murry on Keats," *D. H. Lawrence Review*, 2 (1969), 68–75; to the Johns Hopkins Press for "The Dejection of Coleridge's Ode," *ELH*, 17 (1950), 71–77, and "The Imaginal Design of Shelley's 'Ode to the West Wind,' " *ELH*, 15 (1948), 219–226; to the *Keats-Shelley Journal* for "Image and Imagelessness: A Limited Reading of *Prometheus Bound*," *Keats-Shelley Journal*, 1 (1952), 22–36; to the Modern Language Association for "Keats's 'Ode to a Nightingale,' " *PMLA*, 68 (1953), 211–222; to the National Council of Teachers of English for "The Romantic Unity of *Kubla Khan*," *College English*, 13 (1951), 13–18; to *New Literary History* for "Hawthorne, Literary History, and Criticism" (original title "Literary History Romanticized"), *New Literary History*, 1 (1970), 237–247; to the Regents of the University of California for "*Billy Budd*: The Order of the Fall," *Nineteenth-Century Fiction*, 15 (1960), 189–205, copyright 1960 by the Regents of the University of California; to *Style* for "Weird Mockery: An Element of Hawthorne's Style," *Style*, 2 (1968), 191–201; to Tulane University for "Coleridge's Conversation Poems," *Tulane Studies in English*, 5 (1955), 103–110; "The Genre of *The Ancient Mariner*," *TSE*, 7 (1957), 111–124; "The Themes of Melville's Later Poetry," *TSE*, 10 (1960), 101–116; "Melville's *Clarel*: Doubt and Belief," *TSE*, 11 (1961), 65–86; and "Melville's Poetry," *TSE*, 12 (1962), 81–86.

With Love to my Daughters,
Catherine Harter and Faith Underhill Fogle

Table of Contents

Introduction ix

1 Hawthorne, Literary History, and Criticism   1
2 Coleridge's Conversation Poems   17
3 The Genre of *The Ancient Mariner*   27
4 The Romantic Unity of *Kubla Khan*   43
5 The Dejection of Coleridge's Ode   53
6 The Imaginal Design of Shelley's *Ode to the West Wind*   60
7 Image and Imagelessness   69
   A LIMITED READING OF *PROMETHEUS UNBOUND*
8 Dante and Shelley's *Adonais*   87
9 Keats's *Ode to a Nightingale*   100
10 Beauty and Truth   116
   JOHN MIDDLETON MURRY ON KEATS
11 Weird Mockery   124
   AN ELEMENT OF HAWTHORNE'S STYLE
12 The Themes of Melville's Later Poetry   137
13 Melville's *Clarel*   165
   DOUBT AND BELIEF

14 Melville's Poetry   184

15 *Billy Budd*   191
     THE ORDER OF THE FALL

    Notes   210

    Index   219

Introduction

These essays represent my chief critical interests over the past thirty years. As a whole they try to explain the integrity and the artistic responsibility of nineteenth-century romantic poetry and poetic theory, with some heed to the fiction of Hawthorne and of Melville. Explications of Coleridge's *Conversation Poems, Kubla Khan, Dejection: An Ode,* and *The Rime of the Ancient Mariner* emphasize "the reconciliation of opposites," inseparable from organic unity and the romantic creed of imagination. My treatment of *The Ancient Mariner* focuses upon Coleridge's characteristic and omnipresent concern with the responsibilities of the romantic poet, with particular reference to poetic or dramatic truth, and correspondingly the relation of the poet to his audience.

My interpretations of Shelley are to a degree defenses, since among the English romantic poets Shelley has especially needed defense in the twentieth century. He has repeatedly been condemned by serious and influential critics, on principles that have seemed to me obviously too narrow and sometimes too unliterary to be valid. The experience has taught me the limitations of critical controversy, perhaps the limitations of critical dialectic—not neglecting the possibility that the source of the difficulty could be my own limitations as a controversialist. Defense can never quite square with the attack, exposure of fallacy and heresy too frequently entraps into countererrors. I have sought, however, to uncover the real qualities of Shelley's poetry in several of his major poems.

The universally beloved Keats does not require to be defended, but his poetry is not universally understood. Without sacrificing the sense of his wonderful richness and intensity, I endeavor to follow for a little way the complex and vital convolutions of his thought in the *Ode to a Nightingale*, and to demonstrate his urbanity and what I choose to call his "romantic wit." The great odes of Keats are not linear, nor on the other hand sharply antithetical. Their unity is an organic unity, their movement a harmony of movements. John Middleton Murry has come tantalizingly close to catching the living music and the motion of Keats's poetic thought, although at the last it eludes him.

My brief essay on the style of Hawthorne treats him implicitly as a romantic, but as a romantic with a unique flavor, inhabiting alone his chosen place between the imagination and the fancy, maintaining his balance of sympathy and cautious reserve. My approach to Melville's poetry is also fundamentally romantic, since it looks to the romantic poets for comparison and illustration. It is modified, however, by its subject. Melville at his best is breathtaking, almost, one would say, superhuman. But his best is infrequent, his average is interesting but uneven, and his worst is ridiculous. The body of his poetry is organic in that the whole is more impressive than the sum of its parts. It is vital, it succeeds in expressing Melville the genius. In most of his individual poems, on the other hand, it is not possible to look confidently for the complex relationships of organic unity and form. I have therefore not done so. These remarks have some bearing also upon my treatment of *Billy Budd*, an unquestioned masterpiece. The "inner narrator" whom some critics find in *Billy*, a consummate ironist who means the opposite of what he says, is invisible to me, and I can report no more than the results of what I claim to be my anxious and oft-repeated scrutiny of the words of the text, allowing also for the textual problems involved. A critic, like an imaginative writer, should use all he knows. He has no right, however, to go beyond his *assimilated* and therefore organic knowledge and the real registration of his sensibility.

In Chapter 1 below I say something of the literary theory underlying my practical criticism and interpretation, and of my conception of English and American romanticism, as it applies to criticism. Most of the following essays are "explications," often of individual poems or stories. Explication has at present come to be less regarded in academic circles than it used to be. For this there are no doubt various reasons, including sheer reaction from a trend. Explication, however, or, since the word implies exhaustive analysis it may be better to say concrete interpretation, provides the closest and most vital contact with literature. It is an aesthetic imitation, at one further remove from "reality" than its artistic object, and one step closer to discursive reasoning. As imitation it is creative, insofar as it fuses its object with the different mind of the interpreter, with his different experience and associations. He says what seems to him most relevant about his object, and tries to convey his sense of its wholeness and conformation. He is governed by the limitations of the associations of individual words in relation to the work as a whole: he is not to explore all possible associations, but only those that are actually appropriate in the literary circumstances. On this point obviously no positive rule can be formulated, but the problem is one aspect of the general problem of the relationship of part to whole. One mark of an inexperienced interpreter is overreading. He finds more meaning in the individual work than its limits allow of, misapplying his knowledge.

A poem is a fixed object in that (disregarding textual criticism) its words are invariable. But as soon as we interpret we

must bring in our sense of the poet, not in a literal and biographical but in a general and imaginative notion of him. Without this his words fall apart. Without a guiding concept of unity
we are lost, and we cannot conceive this unity without the vital
presence of the poet as the mind behind the words. Analyses of
particulars, or predetermined methods, are in themselves incompatible with genuine literary reading, though they may be
adapted to it. And without a central principle, or our sense of
the poet, elaborate explication falls of its own weight as a whole.
The experience of explicating word-for-word, especially with
poetry, will uncover to us great complexities, but to describe a
structure intelligibly one has to find balances of relative gener-
alities. In writing of romantic literature it is particularly necessary to avoid the gap between extremes of unity and variety, of
generality and particularity, as will be seen in the following
chapter.

With these views in mind I have always sought to make my
interpretations central, vital, and pertinent: that is, to preserve
in all cases the distinction between the poem or story and what
is useful to say about it; and to be faithful to my own sense of
the life-principle of my object. I try neither to exhaust the work
nor to second-guess its author, and I write about nothing that
I do not as a whole admire. In this final respect I differ, in theory
at least, with the New Criticism, which sets out to explain
definitively the difference between good and bad literature,
with the consequent obligation of demonstrating badness at
length. It has become customary to say that the new critics are
dead, though the sayers are usually those who hope they are
dead. These pages here and there reflect my own quarrels with
them in the days of their widest influence. They were oversuc-
cessful, and no doubt have been partially absorbed, having done
their work. As critics, however, they remain the most able prac-
titioners who have ever made real contact with academic life,
including the dust and heat of the classroom. Whatever their
defects of theory, they have genuinely cared for the values of
imaginative literature, and they have been sufficiently well-
educated to express their values and opinions incisively. The

New Criticism, as distinguished from individual new critics, has failed as all movements must fail, because it is susceptible of being vulgarized into a set of mechanical rules, and this particular failure was located in the new critical pretensions to absolute literary judgment. To my thinking the movement stands convicted of an oversimplified literary history, set forth with tremendous persuasiveness. As regards my own concerns, such arguments as I set forth in defense of Shelley's *West Wind* are still timely, and will remain so at least as long as F. R. Leavis has access to the correspondence pages of the *Times Literary Supplement.*

1

Hawthorne, Literary History, and Criticism

What I can say of Hawthorne and literary history is limited by my conception of literary study as primarily an examination of individual works, based on the fundamental experience of a reader alone with a book. In this conception are involved the implications of Coleridge's oracular dictum "that nothing can permanently please, which does not contain in itself the reason why it is so, and not otherwise." Literary history, that is, is concerned with imaginative literature, whose purposes lie in itself. Coleridge also says that "the office of philosophical *disquisition* consists in just *distinction;* while it is the privilege of the philosopher to preserve himself constantly aware, that distinction is not division." In other words there is no necessary division between literary history and criticism, though there is a distinction. They cannot be practised simultaneously, but each must continually bear in mind the legitimate claims of the other.

There is, then, no absolute distinction (thus no division)

between the critical and the historical approach. Writing about Hawthorne's fiction in the context of a large and steadily increasing body of critical and historical scholarship, I feel obliged to explain myself as best I can. I am writing directly about Hawthorne's texts, but implicitly in the light of biography and a generally historical conception of his period and environment, with more than usual regard to his English in addition to his American literary relationships. I aspire to objectivity, and to critical principles that are universally valid. Neither aspiration is attainable without historical perspective, and in a sense neither is attainable at all. A critic interprets, and he cannot escape his own beliefs and viewpoint, which must dictate what he sees. Yet his limitation is also his life and his value, so long as his object is still the works he assesses and expounds, and his results will be the only truths that literary criticism can and should produce.

Criticism, as I think of it, strives to fuse author and critic, and to reconcile permanent critical principles with the temporal relativism of history. Relativism is the basis of history, a great and massive fact, perhaps a barrier. A theory of literary history should, however, be organic, not fixed. Its scheme should be flexible; the chronological limitations imposed by some conscientious historians are unnecessarily hampering. It is reductive, for instance, to interpret a man's writing exclusively in the light of what he has said up to the time of writing, in a kind of legalism that confines us to courtroom rules of evidence, although positively chronological order can elicit continuity and vital coherence. Those who have paid close heed to the dating of Hawthorne's tales, for example, have frequently been rewarded by a view of novel and interesting relationships. In his case, however, the dating of the early stories and sketches is unusually difficult, and in any event there is less development to observe in Hawthorne than in most writers. Still more important for the critic, close heed to external relationships is incompatible with full and sympathetic attention to the individual work as a living, unique entity, sufficient to itself. One cannot do everything at once.

2

Unlike our powerful purists of literary interpretation, I admit biography into my critical scheme. A critic may say in his wrath that all biographers are liars since they tell us things they cannot possibly know and lure us on to accept these as truths. In biography as elsewhere the facts of research are indispensable, but as means, not ends, and they are conclusive of nothing but themselves. Only as they are transformed do they become valuable, and they remain complex and mobile in their transformation. There is, for instance, the celebrated isolation of both Hawthorne and Melville from American society. After his graduation from Bowdoin in 1825 Hawthorne shut himself up for twelve years in his room. Melville withdrew from his hopes and his career before 1860, and we imagine him a haughty recluse, whose soul was like a star and dwelt apart. In his fine biography Randall Stewart tries to disperse the Hawthorne legend by the facts: Hawthorne saw people and had social engagements during these twelve years of his; his isolation was not literal. And if we look at the chronicle of day-to-day living in Jay Leyda's *Melville Log* we find that our recluse had far too much family for literal loneliness: wife, children, brothers, sisters, in-laws, cousins, uncles, aunts, Melvilles, Gansevoorts, Shaws, with whom he was in constant contact, and who treated the great *isolato* with disconcerting matter-of-factness. Yet Hawthorne's isolation was an all-important fact to himself, to which he adverted over many years; and Melville's spiritual loneliness was constant.

A human life is almost infinitely complex, whether it is considered as internal or external, and the fullest conceivable biography can only be an abstract of it; the "facts" leave a wide area open to interpretation. Byron was accustomed to laugh at his imaginative self-projection of the Byronic hero, and at those who took it literally and were awed (or hostile) when confronted with the man himself; not that his image was false, but rather that it was only part of the truth about him. He remarked how many moments, how many shades of consciousness, how many activities go into the making of a single day, and asked how as Byronic hero he could ever have managed the daily process of shaving. The literary historian as biographer needs to adopt a mode of thought that recognizes the limitations of "objective facts," along with the inferences he draws from them.

Hawthorne's life, like his writings, presents suggestive and stimulating complications. He has been portrayed as a haunted misanthrope and as a cheerful and devoted husband and father; as a withdrawn spectator, and also as a lover of the warm domestic hearth. His good friend Herman Melville saw him as a man with a tragic secret, a view that aroused amused astonishment in his son Julian. It is natural, then, that he has attracted many to the challenge of solving his mystery.

His career was symbolic; as Keats said of Shakespeare, he "led a life of Allegory: his works are the comments on it." Its events have a pattern: they move consistently between opposite poles of contraction and expansion, of "withdrawal and return," in a design that was formed at least partly from within by the nature of the man. The pattern was to be carried throughout Hawthorne's life, as he widened his horizons abroad but returned to New England and Concord. His death itself, peaceful but mysterious, on a journey, not unaccompanied yet outward bound to the mountains, is consistent with the whole design.

Literary history is often understood to be the study of parallels between works, usually with the intention of proving the indebtedness of one writer to another. Here one may recur to Coleridge's saying "that nothing can permanently please, which does not contain within itself the reason why it is so, and not otherwise." Surely no writer survives, or is worth serious discussion, who can be analyzed into his sources as a product of causes external to himself. This is not to say that the study of sources and influences and trends is without value—not at all. But these are lifeless and meaningless if they are detached from their vital centers: the writer, his writings, and their interfusion.

I am suggesting that the truths of literature are essentially metaphorical, and correspondingly that the truths to be found in literary parallels and "sources" are also metaphorical. W. K.

Wimsatt, at the end of his monumental essay on "The Structure of the 'Concrete Universal' in Literature," in which he patiently explores the possibilities of attaining to an objective criticism of poetry, comes to the conclusion that the meaning of poetry, like the meaning of metaphor, is like "the square root of two, or like π, which cannot be expressed by rational numbers, but only as their limit. Criticism is like 1.414 . . . or 3.1416 . . . , not all it would be, yet all that can be had and very useful." In the "Tentative Conclusion" to his *Anatomy of Criticism*, Northrop Frye asserts that "pure literature, like pure mathematics, contains its own meaning." Pursuing his analogy, he arrives at a sweeping speculation: "is it true that the verbal structures of psychology, anthropology, theology, history, law, and everything else built out of words have been informed or constructed by the same kind of myths and metaphors that we find, in their original form, in literature?"

Having incautiously invoked Frye, I am now obliged to exorcise him (if I can) as too mighty a magician for my limited purpose, who is willing to prove a great deal more than I want of him—which is merely to say, as above, that the truths to be gotten from comparing passages to each other, as the basic act of studying parallels and sources, have consequences that are merely or essentially metaphorical. As with the confrontation of the metaphorical poles of tenor and vehicle, the comparison fertilizes, and an indefinable truth appears as an outer limit, a tertium quid, or Wimsatt's irrational number that reaches towards infinity. There is admittedly a difference both in medium and intent between poetic metaphor and the act of comparing that constitutes source study. External evidence can be adduced in the latter case, for one thing, as a helpful presumption. Yet the ultimate purposes should be the same.

Thus, for example, the case of Hawthorne and the English romantic poets. There is unquestionably a relationship here, which should increase our knowledge of the ties between nineteenth-century English and American romanticism. External evidence exists of Hawthorne's acquaintance with Wordsworth, Coleridge, Byron, Shelley, and Keats, in reading lists and in the records of his book withdrawals from the Salem Athenaeum. He refers to them directly, too, in his fiction and his notebooks. Here, then, is a basis of facts, in the root sense of *facta*, things that have been made and are definite. Yet any formulation we arrive at by this means, to place Hawthorne between American and English romanticism, will be metaphorical. By bringing the two together in him we ought to be able to enrich both, and to achieve a fuller conception of romanticism itself.

Students have expended much effort to determine how much and in what respects Hawthorne should be called a romantic. This quest can lead to a dead end in barren legalism and logic-chopping; judiciously conducted, however, it should help to define something unique about his art, a special poignancy added to his Puritanism and Augustanism, and unexplained by either. In particular it should clarify the sense in which his fictional art is poetic. Correspondingly it ought to show his "poetics," that is, his theory of the romance, in a wider perspective than American students have envisaged, and thus help to place Hawthorne better in his own time and environment.

If we narrow this problem, returning to its component parts in Hawthorne's apparent contacts with particular passages, we rarely find the certainty of direct reference; Hawthorne was not an allusive writer. One such instance, however, does occur in *The Marble Faun*. Describing the Coliseum by moonlight, he invokes Byron, in such fashion as to emphasize the likelihood of influence. Actually in Byron's poetry there are two famous accounts of the Coliseum: one, very extensive, in canto 4 of *Childe Harold*, the other, briefer but striking, toward the end of *Manfred*. One guesses that Hawthorne drew on both from memory, without rereading either. What is common to Byron and Hawthorne is, first, the symbolic effect of moonlight itself, with a unique imaginative impact, in which the ruin lives again, yet evokes the perspective of time. This leads in turn to reflections upon the mingled grandeur and iniquity of the Rome the Coliseum represents. Yet

Hawthorne remains Hawthornean throughout: moonlight is almost obsessively present in his fiction, and time a favorite theme. His relation to Byron is chiefly metaphorical, not factual, although fact is present in it.

In literary history, as in literary criticism, the problem of value has to be faced. Attempts to dismiss it simply transfer it to something outside literature that the literary historian values more. Without pretending to definitive argument on so difficult and fundamental a question, one might appeal to human nature itself, or "the nature of things," as the ground of value judgments, as Aristotle grounds his aesthetics of imitation in nature and the structure and limits of the human mind; for instance, in what he has to say of magnitude and duration in tragedy. Indeed it is hard to frame a language that is free from expressions of value, as one finds, for example, in the early writings of I. A. Richards, where he was seeking the objectivity of logical positivism.

Northrop Frye has argued persuasively for postponing value judgments until we know as much as possible, in terms of literary history, about the thing and the kind (genre) of thing we are discussing. And who could take exception to this? Yet one wonders, from experience, whether at this rate we shall ever get around to making judgments at all. Frye adduces most telling instances, such as Rymer's notorious critique of *Othello,* of critical fallacies. But Rymer's principles were, first, thoroughly corrupt, and, second, dishonestly applied; his fault was not simply his desire to evaluate. As to genre one may agree with Coleridge that we must carefully distinguish *kind* before we try to determine *degree*, but the differentiation of kind is not an end in itself.

Our assumptions about literary history, as about criticism, should in fact be based on what we find in ourselves, as Aristotle's aesthetics are based on what he found in nature. We wish instinctively to know our subject as a whole, and also to grasp it in parts, even in individuals. We find, of course, that we cannot achieve our goals, and retire defeated, or exhaust ourselves accumulating particulars, or frame large baseless theories, or frankly specialize in some closed-off area of our field. The remedy lies in a large but necessary assumption, which has to be won the hard way through doubts and difficulties: that there *is* a whole, to which one's particular area is organically related; that our studies are grounded in reality and reason; and that they are continuous and consonant with each other.

Henry James, discussing the role of experience in the making of fiction, rejects it in its sense of literal fact. It is good to keep a notebook of one's experiences, but this is not the root of the matter. What is vital is "the power to guess the unseen from the seen, to trace the implication of things, to judge the whole piece by the pattern, the condition of feeling life in general so completely that you are well on your way to knowing any particular corner of it" ("The Art of Fiction"). James is especially apt for my general purposes, since, as Joseph A. Ward has said in his valuable book *The Search for Form*, James reconciled an organic theory and critical vocabulary with a firm conception of structure and detail, in a synthesis itself organic.

An organicist theory best befits the purposes and the processes of literary history, the complex continuity of its subject matter. (My notion of literary organicism evolves from the implications of Coleridge's thought, as I interpret Coleridge's thought.) As with literary history, so also with literary criticism. The nature of literary creation is organic and complex, as is its embodiment in the literary work. Here it may be remarked that we need not outlaw speculation about the writer's creative processes in order to deal with our proper business, the work itself. That is, we can imply the whole, while giving our attention to its most appropriate part. René Wellek's "Perspectivism" represents the proper attitude, and Wellek's application of the parable of the blind men and the elephant is most apt (*A History of Modern Criticism*, 1:vii). The elephant, the thing to be known, is a living whole, and the mistakes of the blind men are failures in inference. Taking too literally the part for the whole, they cannot, in James's words, "trace the implications of things."

Organicism is a powerful enchantress, of most questionable attractions for the unwary. The fascinations of "organic unity" may tempt us to fall into sheer tautology ("A rose is a rose is a rose"), or to yield ourselves to the perfect whole in a manner all too confiding. Melville's remark about Goethe, that it is inappropriate to exhort a man with a raging toothache to "live in the All," has its bearing upon this: the particular can be a most powerful toothache. Certainly a critic should avoid absolute monism, since it tends to be unintelligible though incontrovertible. What one ordinarily fails to find in organicist theory is sufficient attention to diversity, discrimination, and developing from discrimination, gradation; the sense of a structure that is at once living and at the same time firm and distinct in its interrelationships. Such a theory demands inclusiveness, and establishes the principle of dominant emphasis, rather than absolute demarcation. That is, one should emphasize the writing and not the writer, but still find, with Louis Rubin, the teller in the tale. As another consequence of a properly considered theory of organicism, while concepts and categories have their place in the critic's scheme, they are to be regarded as relative and unfixed. They need to prove themselves continually by their contact with individual writers and works, of which they are not the masters but the servants.

Thus, for example, at least two romanticisms have been pointed out in nineteenth-century American literature: the romanticism of Emerson, Thoreau, and the transcendentalists, and the romanticism of Hawthorne, Poe and Melville. Whitman, who belongs with Emerson and Thoreau, disrupts the pattern for those who see the Civil War as a great dividing line for American literature as well as American society. I raise problems without taking responsibility for their solutions, but merely in order to point out that the romanticisms in question are relative to each other and should be relative to a third and larger concept of romanticism, not fixed and absolute in themselves. In addition the customary time divisions are not immutable facts, or banks in which the stream of literature must flow perforce. They must demonstrate their value as metaphors, as centers for the imagination, and the demonstration must be made to imaginative literature. This can of course be done; for

Hawthorne and Melville the Civil War was a latter Fall, an exile from the Eden of the Old Republic. The war may conceivably have killed Hawthorne, and in Melville's poetry it divides, at least in retrospect, a Golden Age of innocence and beauty from a utilitarian Age of Iron.

Romanticism is, as I understand it, a strong sense of potentiality, of the rich possibilities of life, of the world, of the mind. I am no further interested in defining it than literary and aesthetic purposes require. It has nothing to do with original sin, political liberalism (save by association), or pantheism, insofar as these are fixed doctrines. Romanticism intends to be as comprehensive and suggestive—perhaps as poignant—as it possibly can. It emphasizes imagination as a creative and organizing power, and usually implies organicism with its pervasive metaphors of life. It is frequently allied with a creed of nature, both subjective and objective, and uses landscape, or in general the external world, as a symbol of reality. It tries to synthesize thought and feeling: to identify it with feeling alone is an error.

Epistemologically speaking, I cannot quite say that romanticism is a Platonic idea with a precise and unchanging reality, since I have never been admitted to the world of archetypal forms. The position taken here amounts to a cautious and tentative conceptualism. It is clearly inconceivable that the same verbal formula would ever be used twice in defining it, although we can surely reach a provisional agreement or at least an understanding about our notions of romanticism. It will serve, however, as a magnetic pole, or a fixed point of reference; from the critic's point of view even practical, descriptive criticism needs general ideas to give it currency. What has historically been called romanticism has provisional validity, but it should be understood metaphorically, not literally. Thus English romanticism 1798–1832 and American romanticism 1830–1855 are useful formulations, but if we take them for realities we get outside the realms of imaginative literature and literary criticism.

Bearing in mind these limitations, we can say that American romanticism has been associated with transcendentalism, organicism, nationalism, expansivism, naturalism (in its broadest sense), optimism, and antinomianism. Its opponents impugn it for foolish optimism and braggadocio; and some of those scholars who have discerned romantic elements in Hawthorne, such as Millicent Bell in her *Hawthorne's View of the Artist*, have done so with regret. Conversely because of their celebrated "darkness" Hawthorne and Melville have been labelled antiromantics or negative romantics. For many reasons Emerson has been slighted during most of the twentieth century, especially by those who haven't read him, while Hawthorne and Melville have been riding high. More recently there appears to be a counterreaction, which unfortunately requires that Hawthorne be denigrated in order to restore the original Sage of Concord to his rightful place. Contrarily several literary historians have rid Hawthorne of his darkness in order to put him back with Emerson (sometimes with Longfellow) in the broad sunlight of the central American tradition.

Hawthorne, Melville, and Poe can be brought into the romantic fold under the spacious covering of "potentiality." American romanticism as it is generally thought of, in Emerson, Thoreau, and Whitman, has tremendous strength in its monism, and a corresponding weakness, aesthetically speaking, in its application of organicist theory, as also and correspondingly in its conception of symbol, the relation of the part to the whole, the Emersonian each and all. Whether this is simply the inevitable defect of a virtue, or its characteristic configuration or shape, depends on the point of view. At any rate I perceive it as something wanting.

The fault is a too literal identification of microcosm with macrocosm, an undiscriminating trust in the potentialities of the individual symbol, and it results in monotony, circularity, insufficient gradation and modulation. Thus Emerson is inexhaustibly interesting and poetic in his particulars but monotonous in his totalities, from overintensity. At the same time American romanticism has a freshness and vigor that is unique. Hawthorne was tinged with it, as he could hardly fail to have been, as an intelligent man who had also lived in Concord ("Et ego in Arcadia vixi").

English romanticism is more complex, since there were more

notable romantic writers in England than in America, and a more complex literary tradition more immediately available to them. Perhaps, too, as a movement it was less self-conscious, less overtly theoretical, and consequently more varied. Its basic characteristics are the same as the American romantics possessed, with their emphasis upon imagination, organicism, and symbol. The great English romantic poets had on the whole a stronger bent toward psychological introspection and self-revelation, but not as a fixed creed. In their pursuit of potentiality they were inclusive: they looked upwards and outwards as well as within, and it is an error for a critic to view them as systematic in anything but their art.

As with American romanticism, the English romantics sought to envision totality and to find their symbols for it by means of the concrete and particular. This involves the faith that the poetic imagination can envision reality, that beauty and truth, or truth and poetry can be reconciled. The problem for the romantics was to bring the imagination into balance with the understanding or discursive reason, which they felt had come to dominate the mind of modern man. By itself the understanding could give only the dead world of materialism, the abstract world of analysis, the narrow world of custom: Shelley spoke for the romantics in saying, "We want the power to imagine that which we know." Their enemy was not positive evil, but chaos or abstraction, the meaningless particular or the abstract, lifeless system. As Coleridge wrote in *This Lime-Tree Bower My Prison*, "No sound is dissonant which tells of Life."

So too Hawthorne: his fiction may be thought of as romantic poetry in its sense of the beautiful, in its special kind of universality, in its heed to the picturesque, and in its care for harmony and modulation. His special search for reality appears in relation to the picturesque as distinctness of outline. He has the typical romantic regard for imagination. He accepts the famous distinction, most elaborately formulated by Wordsworth and Coleridge, between imagination and fancy, though both in theory and practice he permits the two to run together. In defining his unique quality it is unjust, however, to treat him as a man of flawed or incomplete imagination, since this quality arises from a stress between the sense of the fictional and the sense of truth in his writing. James's treatment of Hawthorne, which emphasizes his fancy and a kind of frivolity in him, is acute in catching his tone, but misled in regarding it as simply an incomplete manifestation of the full and rounded Jacobean harmony.

The American antithesis between nineteenth-century romanticism and realism, between, let us say, Hawthorne and the school of Howells, likewise needs reexamination. Our habit of framing antitheses to provide definitions, as with classic-romantic or symbol-allegory, is unfortunate if it becomes fixed and literal, for each term then limits the other. Also the problem of value creeps in unheralded through the wrong door, and what was intended for definition becomes instead an instrument of exclusion, as in T. E. Hulme's famous essay on "Romanticism and Classicism," where romanticism goes down to ignominious defeat. Perhaps I am merely complaining of an implication that realism is really the closer of the two to reality, which I will by no means admit. My point, however, as with American and English romanticism, is that an antithesis should presuppose its synthesis, or that in other terms we are in actuality dealing with the poles of a metaphor, from which will arise a larger, a verbally indeterminate, and mobile idea.

The process of building an organic theory of literary history can be formulated abstractly in terms of *alternation, consolidation,* and *assimilation.* Alternation involves a due regard for the parts of the subject to be examined. Coleridge, constructing a theory of organic nature, conceived what he called the "law of bicentrality": everything has a center within itself, but also outside of itself. Assuming, perhaps hastily, that this is self-evidently true as a special way of describing the organic relationship of the part to the whole, one would then assert that we should alternate between these centers in contemplating our subject, rather than pass from one to the other without looking back. One illustration of the consequences can be drawn from Coleridge himself, when he defines the poem as "proposing to itself such delight from the *whole,* as is compatible with a distinct gratification from each component part" (*Biographia Literaria*, ch. 14). It follows that metre, though Coleridge is expounding an organicist theory, has its own though subordinate reality and vital center, and can therefore be legitimately examined in itself, while it is yet in the last analysis *assimilated* into the totality of the poem. A more radical organicism, which I would reject, would treat metre as purely expressive, and thus *dissolve* it into the poem. Consolidation is a pause to take stock of the materials, to be sure that they are properly placed before we go on to assimilate them into an organic whole. For literary history, the theory provides a method of organizing comprehensively.

To consolidate requires the right perspective. In trying to find the best, the most comprehensive position, the central object of our pursuit appears to us dynamic, elusive, and even infinite in its possibilities, while other considerations on its periphery are static and finite. Such is ordinarily the case with the literary historian and the critic. The historian assumes that all aesthetic problems have been solved—or that they are insoluble and therefore chimerical—while the possible relations of literature to its environment are endless. The critic, on the other hand, though aware of historical considerations, views them as a fixed and static background only. One solution to this problem might be found in the perspective of Aristotle's *Poetics:* to discuss tragedy we must first determine what is proper to our discussion, amid a wide range of possibilities. Or perhaps, since I cannot claim to be more than momentarily Aristotelian, I must return to the implications of Coleridge's law of bi-centrality, which tries in its organicism to allow for vitally complex relationships, in which due subordination is still preserved within the most comprehensive possible point of view.

My idea of assimilation has this consequence for a theory of literary history, as well as of literary criticism: the center of its subject is imaginative ("creative") literature as it appears in the temporal order of history. General history, sociology, psychology, philosophy, political science are *out*, along with other kinds of knowledge too numerous to mention. This summary act of banishment is essential to establish a center of force, an organizing power. In that case, it may be asked, what becomes of your "assimilation"? Where now is the boasted inclusiveness of your theory?

My answer is in what I have called alternation, or Coleridge's bi-centrality. All knowledge is more or less relevant to literary history, but most of it is peripheral, and in any event significant only from the point of view of the center. Sociology, psychology, philosophy have their own centers, their assumptions, their goals, which are not those of literature. We must, in fact, distinguish to achieve comprehension of the true relationships, while at the same time avoiding absolute division. Furthermore the vital relationships that unquestionably exist will prove to be not factual or fixed, but figurative and ultimately indeterminate.

The ideal goal of literary history and criticism alike is to discern the continuity between past and present, or, as we frequently say, to illuminate the present by means of the past. This is rather the theoretical limit of our quest than what we can actually attain. We may, however, arrive at metaphorical solutions, such as Longinus' conception of literary continuity as a transmitted fire and light, which may be the source of our twentieth-century reconciliation of tradition with originality.

In the *Essay on Criticism* Pope tells us to read the classics in the spirit in which they were written. Thus it is the goal of literary history to connect us organically with our literary past. It often happens, however, that instead a formidable barrier is thrown up between us and the classic; the historian reverses foreground and background, and hides what we have sought to see. The insight of metaphor has on occasion bridged the great gap: such a figure, for example, as T. S. Eliot conceived in "Tradition and the Individual Talent," a positive revelation, at least to the eye of faith:

No poet, no artist of any art, has his complete meaning alone. His significance, his appreciation is the appreciation of his relation to the dead poets and artists. You cannot value him alone; you must set him, for contrast and comparison, among the dead. . . . The necessity that he shall conform, that he shall cohere, is not one-sided; what happens when a new work of art is created is something that happens simultaneously to all the works of art which preceded it. The existing monuments form an ideal order among themselves, which is modified by the introduction of the new (the really new) work of art among them. The existing order is complete before the new work arrives; for order to persist after the supervention of novelty, the *whole* existing order must be, if ever so slightly, altered; and so the relations, proportions, values of each work of art toward the whole are readjusted; and this is conformity between the old and the new. Whoever has approved this idea of order, of the form of European, of English literature will not find it preposterous that the past should be altered by the present as much as the present is directed by the past.

This passage, in a brilliant metaphor, breaks down the barrier between past and present, or perhaps leaps effortlessly over it. It has a sense of the whole, and it assumes what I take to be the most essential beliefs: that it is possible to establish direct contact with a literary work of any period; that literary history has a center as well as a line; and that the work and history are intimately interrelated, like the poles of a metaphor.

2

Coleridge's Conversation Poems

"If we except," says D. G. James in *The Romantic Comedy*, "those poems which have, in varying degree, something of a dream quality—*The Ancient Mariner, Kubla Khan, Christabel*, we see that nearly all Coleridge's poems have a conversational tone.[1] The conversation poems referred to here, however, are those which were specified by George Maclean Harper in his well-known article of 1925:[2] *The Aeolian Harp, Reflections on Having Left a Place of Retirement, This Lime-Tree Bower My Prison, Frost at Midnight, Fears in Solitude, The Nightingale*, and *To William Wordsworth*. This list differs, though, from Harper's in omitting *Dejection: An Ode*, while at the same time it reluctantly defers to his judgment in admitting *To William Wordsworth*, which is separated from the others by eight years' time. The reason for omitting *Dejection* is twofold: first, that it is an irregular Pindaric ode, a form which is not precisely adapted to conversational purposes, and, second, that in its published as distinguished from its original form it is a little too good for the genre of "conversation poem," which is essentially modest and limited in its claims.

Coleridge specifically entitles *The Nightingale* "a conversation poem," and he termed *Reflections on Having Left a Place of Retirement* "a Poem which affects not to be Poetry," later adding the significant motto *Sermoni propriora* ("better suited to talk"), Horace's description of his *Satires* and *Epistles*. Coleridge writes of *Fears in Solitude*, "N.B. The above is perhaps not Poetry,—but rather a sort of middle thing between Poetry and Oratory—sermoni propriora.—Some parts are, I am conscious, too tame even for animated prose."[3] D. G. James attributes this modesty to Coleridge's sense of his shortcomings:

Coleridge felt the impulse to creation; he was also aware, as he states at its extreme in *Dejection*, of a certain failure of imagination, of something negative arresting the flow of his energies. The result was a "sort of middle thing"—a poetry conversational, made thereby unpretentious, and yet revealing its author's unease by lapsing from time to time into a false grandeur, an oratorical manner; poetry written almost apologetically, yet also, too frequently, absurdly grandiose. Thus he is either "affecting" not to write poetry or being excessively "poetical."[4]

These acute remarks are cited not for purposes of refutation, but for amplification and to some extent for circumvention. The conversation poems have not the intensity of great poetry, while it is true that viewed in a certain light certain lines and phrases leap out from their context as uncomfortable instances of "false grandeur": such a passage as this, for instance:

Praise, praise it, O my Soul! oft as thou scann'st
The sluggard Pity's vision-weaving tribe!
Who sigh for Wretchedness, yet shun the Wretched,
Nursing in some delicious solitude
Their slothful loves and dainty sympathies!
I therefore go, and join head, heart, and hand,
Active and firm, to fight the bloodless fight

Of Science, Freedom, and the Truth in Christ.

(On Having Left a Place of Retirement, ll. 54–62)

It was Charles Lamb, I believe, who unkindly translated Coleridge's *propriora sermoni* as "properer for a sermon" (as well as violently objecting to his own sanctification as "gentle-hearted Charles" in *This Lime-Tree Bower My Prison*) and such lines as these point up the aptness of the jest. They are not empty, the thought contained in them indeed is serious and crucial; but the style, with its artful Miltonic inversions, its abstract pseudo-personifications, its elaborate arrangement, is utterly inappropriate. The ideas would be best expressed in the neutral style of sustained argument, where difficulty demands clarity.

Thus if one places certain demands upon the conversation poems he will find them wanting. Yet they are fine poetry nevertheless, if not great poetry, and the disabilities which James attaches to them are susceptible of kinder and perhaps more profitable explanation than he provides. Discussion of their presumed defects will lead, one hopes, to a clearer notion of their positive qualities. First, Coleridge's conception of the type of conversation poem, which James interprets as a kind of defense mechanism to conceal his own shortcomings, is dignified by its close relationship to Coleridge's whole way of thinking about poetry. Poetry for him is of many kinds, all in themselves good. Badness consists not in the type, but in the failure to conform to the type's requirements. It is widely believed that Coleridge banished the idea of genre with his theory of organic unity; nothing, however, could be more mistaken than this notion. It is true that genre in Coleridge is not the neo-Aristotelian genre of neoclassicism, predetermined, absolute, deductive, and structurally atomic. But his critical vocabulary makes large use of *genus, species, class,* and *kind,* and he is always willing to grant to others whatever indulgence he asks for himself. The first duty of the critic, in his theory, is not to judge, but to find out what he is dealing with, to determine what principles are genuinely applicable to the object. "Do not," he says to John Thelwall, at the same general period in which he wrote the conversation poems, "let us introduce an Act of Uniformity against Poets."[5] Much later, in Chapter 1 of the *Biographia Literaria*, he makes apology to "Mr. Pope and his followers" for his failure to do them justice. "I was not blind to the merits of this school, yet as from inexperience of the world, and consequent want of sympathy with the general subjects of these poems, they gave me little pleasure, I doubtless undervalued the *kind*, and with the presumption of youth withheld from its masters the legitimate name of poets."[6] With this respect for the kind is associated also the doctrine of inseparability of faults and virtues, from which reviewers to this day might profit much. How often do we still see a book condemned for the very qualities which give it identity and life, not to say form and intelligibility? "I have room enough in *my* brain," writes Coleridge to Thelwall, "to admire, aye, and almost equally, the *head* and fancy of Akenside, and the heart and fancy of Bowles, the solemn lordliness of Milton, and the divine chit-chat of Cowper. And whatever a man's excellence is, that will be likewise his fault."[7] Again, in a passage against review-criticism in the *Biographia*, he states, "I know nothing that surpasses the vileness of deciding on the merits of a poet or painter, not by characteristic defects; for where there is genius, *these* always point to his characteristic *beauties;* but, by accidental failures or faulty passages."[8]

Against the charge of false grandeur one may affirm that it is a defect in the conversation poems of their characteristic virtues. Coleridge is anticipating *Lines Written Above Tintern Abbey* and *The Prelude* by attributing dignity and significance to the subjective meditations of a private person in unremarkable, even homely circumstances: lying on a hilltop, for example, or sitting alone by a dying fire with a baby asleep beside him, as in *Frost at Midnight*, or sitting in a garden while his friends are enjoying a walk, because his wife has accidentally spilt a skillet of boiling milk on his foot, as in *This Lime-Tree Bower My Prison*. He is in the process of developing a new poetic attitude and a new kind of poem, and it is little wonder if his hand sometimes strikes a false note, like Wordsworth in the *Ode on Intimations of Immortality* with his

Behold the Child among his new-born blisses,
A six years' Darling of a pigmy size!

Like Coleridge, Wordsworth is still in the process of formulating a new attitude and subject matter.

The conversation poems are romantic efforts to combine naturalness with dignity and significance. They are deliberately minor, but most of them are masterpieces of their minor kind. The emotions they convey are gentle, quietistic, delicately modulated. They are comparable to the more formal eighteenth-century poem of meditation in the tradition of Thomson, Akenside, Blair, Young, Gray, and Collins on the one hand, but modified on the other by the graceful informality of Horace's *Epistles* and *Satires,* while they contain feelings about nature and subjective experience which are unique and novel. These poems in some degree exploit the random associative processes of a relaxed mind, in order to add a new dimension and possibility to poetic subject matter. Thus the apparently unfixed musings of *Frost at Midnight,* in which the mind from sheer vacuity at length focuses on the grate, or the luxurious musing of *The Aeolian Harp,* as undirected as the harp's own windblown melodies.

It is necessary to distinguish, however. The conversation poems imitate naturalness and spontaneity without being literally spontaneous and natural. They are carefully wrought artifacts, and they are a long way from modern experiments in the stream of consciousness and automatic writing. They have a center and a centrality, which generally come from a central philosophical idea used as a counterpoint to the concrete psychological experience which makes the poem's wholeness and life. Such is the conception of totality, "the One Life," in *The Aeolian Harp* and *This Lime-Tree Bower My Prison,* or of beneficent nature in *Frost at Midnight.* Coleridge's peculiar faculty of organizing concrete psychological experience around a philosophical center is glanced at frequently in his own comments on his early poetry: "My philosophical opinions are blended with or deduced from my feelings, and this, I think, peculiarises my style of writing, and, like everything else, it is sometimes a beauty and sometimes a fault."[9] Ironically this blend of thought and feelings was early advanced against him as a poet, and later as a philosopher.

The conversation poems are written in blank verse, for naturalness and for dignity as well. Like most nondramatic blank verse after Milton this measure is Miltonic, but lowered from Milton by Coleridge's characteristic softness, euphony, and flow. It is still, however, more like Milton than Wordsworth's comparable verse; it is more elaborately varied, more consciously artful, with an occasional "turn," and even in one instance a refrain, the repeated "gentle-hearted Charles" of *This Lime-Tree Bower My Prison:* a tribute to which the ungrateful Charles replied contumaciously, "For God's sake, don't make me ridiculous any more by terming me gentle-hearted in print. ... It almost always means poor-spirited." The effect, indeed, verges on bathos, an example of incautious excess in a legitimate attempt to convey the mood of quiet, delicate solemnity.

The conversation poems have one overarching theme, the romantic vision of unity and life, and one aspiration, for blessedness and peace. They are predominantly poems of internal experience, but this experience is communicable largely by the hieroglyphic symbolism of visible nature. In 1798 Coleridge writes to his brother George, "I devote myself to such works as encroach not on the anti-social passions—in poetry, to elevate the imagination and set the affections in right tune by the beauty of the inanimate impregnated as with a living soul by the presence of life. ... I love fields and woods and mountains with almost a visionary fondness."[10] The passage marks out the fundamental credo of romanticism with masterful conciseness. In a letter to Thelwall he asserts that "My mind feels as if it ached to behold and know something *great*, something *one* and *indivisible*. And it is only in the faith of that that rocks or waterfalls, mountains or caverns, give me the sense of sublimity or majesty! But in this faith *all things* counterfeit infinity."[11] And he goes on to quote some lines from his own *Lime-Tree Bower*,

> I stand
> Silent, with swimming sense; and gazing round
> On the wide landscape, gaze till all doth seem
> Less gross than bodily, a living Thing
> Which acts upon the mind and with such hues
> As clothe th'Almighty Spirit, where He makes
> Spirits perceive His presence!

Here he rises to the realm of the *Ding-an-sich* of absolute reality, where material and ideal are reconciled in pure Being, where the symbol becomes its own meaning. The conversational poems do not generally fly so high, though there are other comparable passages. More usual, however, are verses which at once convey and aspire to a simpler, more tranquil blessedness:

> My pensive Sara! thy soft cheek reclined
> Thus on mine arm, most soothing sweet it is
> To sit beside our Cot, our Cot o'ergrown
> With white-flower'd Jasmin, and the broad-leav'd Myrtle,
> (Meet emblems they of Innocence and Love!)
> And watch the clouds, that late were rich with light,
> Slow saddening round, and mark the star of eve
> Serenely brilliant (such should wisdom be)
> Shine opposite! How exquisite the scents
> Snatch'd from yon bean-field! and the world *so* hush'd!
> The stilly murmur of the distant Sea
> Tells us of silence.
>
> (*The Aeolian Harp*, ll. 1–12)

A cottage, innocence and love, twilight and the evening star, a hush accentuated by the distant murmur of the sea—all is a muted harmony. This poem, *The Aeolian Harp*, is an instance of the manner in which a philosophical idea both blends with and at the same time counterpoints a concrete psychological experience, in one of Coleridge's characteristic reconciliations of opposites. Amid this tranquil hush become audible the soft notes of the aeolian harp in the cottage window, its strings just stirred by the breeze; and this music, perceptible only in quietude, in turn imperceptibly raises the argument of the poem. The harp is the voice of totality:

O, the one Life within us and abroad,
Which meets all motion and becomes its soul,
A light in sound, a sound-like power in light,
Rhythm in all thought, and joyance every where.

(ll. 26–29)

This conception leads on to another speculation, compounded of the unity which the harp expresses and the duality of which this unity is made, for the sound is the product both of instrument and player:

And what if all of animated nature
Be but organic Harps diversely framed,
That tremble into thought, as o'er them sweeps
Plastic and vast, one intellectual breeze,
At once the Soul of each, and God of all?

(ll. 43–48)

But this daring speculation, which has arisen from a deliberate self-surrender to passive quietude, is a violation of the mood which engendered it. The peace of the opening passage is the reward for the innocence of receptivity, with the poet become for the moment even as a little child. This state of mind, at least in *The Aeolian Harp*, depends upon setting the mind to rest, not waking it up. Its harmony derives from acceptance of orthodox belief—as A. E. Housman says, "Earth and high Heaven are fixed of old and founded strong"—not from destroying the Christian cosmos and rebuilding it from Neoplatonic blueprints. So Coleridge retires from his advanced position to the

24

point from which he reached it, back to the innocence of feeling alone:

Well hast thou said and holily disprais'd
These shapings of the unregenerate mind;
Bubbles that glitter as they rise and break
On vain Philosophy's aye-babbling spring.
For never guiltless may I speak of him,
The Incomprehensible! save when with awe
I praise him, and with Faith that inly *feels*.

(ll. 54–60)

One tends to forget that the romantic poem of subjective meditation, if it is successful, is a work of art, a structure with some kind of completed action, with progression, gradation, and balance. Probably the author wishes us to forget, since his purpose is to imitate life directly, to penetrate the heart by immediacy and sincerity of feeling. The ancient mariner has undoubtedly achieved the happy situation for which the romantic poet yearns and burns:

He holds him with his glittering eye—
The Wedding-Guest stood still,
And listens like a three years' child:
The Mariner hath his will.

Yet the means by which he attains his results are frequently artful, with the art which conceals art. In almost all the conversation poems Coleridge passes through an entire movement, with a beginning, a middle, and an end. His progress is usually circular, but he returns to the starting point with much of value which he has amassed along the way: his ending is not merely a return but also a synthesis. We have noticed that *The Aeolian Harp* establishes a state of mind, passes beyond it almost imperceptibly, and then with something of dramatic shock returns to it again. So *Frost at Midnight*, the nearest to perfection of the conversation group, begins with a state of abnormal quietude, moves away from it by means of the one visible object in motion, the fluttering "stranger" on the hearth, a piece of half-burnt paper, develops the "stranger's" associations, and by means of these curves slowly back to a different and fuller quiet, only completed, with really exquisite art, in the final line:

Whether the summer clothe the general earth
With greenness, or the redbreast sit and sing
Betwixt the tufts of snow on the bare branch
Of mossy apple-trees, while the nigh thatch
Smokes in the sun-thaw; whether the eave-drops fall
Heard only in the trances of the blast,
Or if the secret ministry of frost
Shall hang them up in silent icicles,
Quietly shining to the quiet moon.

This effect is attained by careful revision; the first publication, in 1798, contained six more lines at the end, which destroy the effect. So also *The Aeolian Harp*, which appears to represent a single homogeneous experience, is actually a composite of different experiences and was written on two definitely separate occasions.[12] A glance at the variant texts of all the conversation poems tells the same story of careful, painstaking amplification, condensation, and continual recasting to achieve in romantic art the fulness and spontaneity of life.

3

The Genre of *The Ancient Mariner*

The Rime of the Ancient Mariner is in kind a romantic poem, in the special sense in which Coleridge calls *The Tempest* a romantic drama—a poem of purest imagination, as free as the imagination can make it from the trammels of time and space. A number of the difficulties which have bothered the critics of *The Ancient Mariner* can, I think, be diminished if not dispersed by Coleridge's own criticism. His own statements illuminate the problems of its purpose and of the appropriateness of the "moral," the question of the "pure imagination" and of the dream sequence and structure. This is not to say, of course, that the poem can be accounted for through Coleridge's critical theory; the poem and the criticism are, however, in accord, so that it is useful to put them together. And one can do quite well without any reference to laudanum.

Coleridge's lecture on *The Tempest* contains one of his fullest statements on "the romantic." The romantic genre has laws, which we must comprehend before we judge it. All drama must be probable and natural, but Coleridge reminds us that drama is imitation, not literal copy:[1] "that a certain quantum of difference is essential to the former, and an indispensable condition and cause of the pleasure we derive from it." Still there is an improbability which is beyond the pale. This reflection introduces the topic of dramatic illusion.

Illusion is the ideal receptive condition for the theatre audience, and for the reader. This state of illusion is best explained on the analogy of dream, since "our state when we are dreaming differs from that in which we are in the perusal of a deeply interesting novel in the degree rather than in the kind." This kind of illusion, however, differs significantly from the illusion of dream, since it depends first upon the skill of the creator[2] and, second, upon the voluntary assent of audience or reader. "We are brought up to this point, as far as it is requisite or desirable, gradually, by positive aidance of our own will. We *choose* to be deceived." All other excellencies are "means to this chief end, that of producing and supporting this willing illusion." Finally the romantic drama is a kind "the interests of which are independent of all historical facts and associations, and arise from their fitness to that faculty of our nature, the imagination I mean, which owes no allegiance to time and place,—a species of drama, therefore, in which errors in chronology and geography, no mortal sins in any species, are venial and count for nothing."[3]

The romantic, then, must reconcile the probable with the improbable. This opposition is resolved most fundamentally by making a distinction between essence and accident: a surface unlikelihood will disappear within a deeper truth.[4] As Coleridge says of his share in the *Lyrical Ballads*, "the excellence aimed at was to consist in the interesting of the affections by the dramatic truth of such emotions, as would naturally accompany such situations, supposing them real."[5] Essential probability and truth must be maintained; and the artist must avoid such improbabilities as are harmful to his effect of illusion. "Whatever tends to prevent the mind from placing it [self] or from being gradually placed in this state in which the images have a negative reality must be a defect, and consequently anything that must force itself on the auditors' mind as improbable, not because it *is* improbable (for that the whole play is foreknown to be) but because it cannot but *appear* as such."[6]

The romantic is the voice of the pure imagination, unaided by extraneous or accidental advantages. As the voice of imagination, it represents the purest beauty, the most consummate artistry, while it represents also the purest truth, purged of the dross of the merely material, and akin to the ultimate truths of the transcendental reason:

> The romantic poetry . . . appealed to the imagination rather than to the senses and to the reason as contemplating our inward nature, the workings of the passions in their most retired recesses. . . . The reason is aloof from time and space; the imagination [has] an arbitrary control over both; and if only the poet have such power of exciting our internal emotions as to make us present to the scene in imagination chiefly, he acquires the right and privilege of using time and space as they exist in the imagination, obedient only to the laws which the imagination acts by.[7]

"The reason is aloof from time and space," while for Coleridge the lower faculty of understanding is the slave of time and space. The imagination has "an arbitrary control over both"; it is the mediator and reconciler of reason and understanding, and performs an indispensable mental function. Dealing with the materials, the appearance which reason scorns, it infuses them nevertheless with the truth of reason; it *idealizes* them, as far as it is able. "It dissolves, diffuses, dissipates, in order to recreate; or where this process is rendered impossible, yet still at all events it struggles to idealize and to unify."[8] (This suggestion of struggle is important, since it expresses the mediate post of the imagination, its middle ground between image and idea.)

For Coleridge, then, "pure imagination" has no connotations of triviality. The imagination is an intensely serious faculty. The romantic literature of the imagination is a genius struggling to create, not a kitten leaping at its shadow. Undeniably, however, there is more than an element of play in the romantic imagination, and certainly in *The Ancient Mariner*. "A poem is that species of composition, which is opposed to works of science, by proposing for its immediate object, pleasure, not truth."[9] The imagination delights in its own powers. It prides itself upon its independence of artificial aids of "realism," the petty verisimilitude of literal imitation, which Coleridge names "copy." Much, in fact, of this distinctive quality of the Coleridgean romantic poem is attributable to this feeling for power, at once desired and self-realized. *The Ancient Mariner* is quite precisely a tour de force, while it is yet intensely serious. The romantic poet seeks power—over his audience and himself as well. Coleridge's doctrine of illusion, with its analogy to dream, is the prescription for this power, a magic white and beneficent. The effect of romantic poetry should be what the poet of *Kubla Khan* aspires to:

I would build that dome in air!
That sunny dome! those caves of ice!

This romantic poetry would be the opposite of austere. It aims at a rich[10] overflow of pleasure and wonder, from image, idea, and sound. Whatever restraints the poet must actually exercise, none should be perceptible in his poem. There is an ever-present distrust of the prima facie attractive, of which contemporary taste has more perhaps than its fair share. We can hardly accept poetry as serious unless it upsets our ears by discords, our feelings by obvious ironies. Young poets are required to be bitter before they have had a fair chance to acquire a flavor at all. The romantic poem of the imagination will undoubtedly not satisfy such requirements.

The motto prefixed to *The Ancient Mariner* is amazingly apposite to the central problem of the romantic. "Facile credo," it begins, "plures esse Naturas invisibiles quam visibiles in rerum universitate." Here is the vitalist idealism which is the heart of all romantic thought—the sense of unseen and mysterious life, and the faith, "Facile credo," which is necessary to perceive it. Imagination "is essentially *vital*, even as all objects (*as* objects) are essentially fixed and dead."[11] The opposite to this affirmation, however, is posed in the next two sentences: "Sed horum omnium familiam quis nobis enarrabit? et gradus et cognationes et discrimina et singulorum munera?" It is the hard task of the romantic poet to imagine the unimaginable, to give to airy nothing a local habitation, and a name, complete with *familiam, gradus, cognationes, discrimina,* and *munera.* In short he must number the streaks of the Blue Flower, he must order the exciting intuitions of the ideal into process, gradation, and hierarchy. "You speak," says Keats, "of Lord Byron and me. There is this great difference between us: he describes what he sees—I describe what I imagine. Mine is the hardest task."[12]

It is pleasant, continues the motto, to contemplate the image of a greater and better world: "ne mens assuefacta hodiernae vitae minutiis se contrahat nimis, et tota subsidat in pusillas cogitationes." Again a basic tenet of romanticism: awaken the mind from its sloth of custom, that it may perceive the marvels which crowd around it. And yet again the qualification so typical of Coleridge himself, the statement of the necessary opposite. "Sed veritati interea invigilandum est, modusque servandus, ut certa ab incertis, diem a nocte, distinguamus." Measure and bound must be preserved, the certain distinguished from the doubtful. Voyaging on strange seas of thought, the Coleridgean explorer makes prudent provision, and takes notes on his experiences. Coleridge is in a sense the supreme rationalist, who forces intelligence to its outermost bounds, while at the same time distinguishing "certa ab incertis" with exquisite solicitude. So, in fact, must the great magicians of the romantic always be. It takes a strong head and a sense of direction to travel on such seas. No one has yet, I think, fittingly described the extent of conscious artistry, the judgment, taste, and self-possession which went into *The Eve of St. Agnes,* or the *Christabel* or *Kubla Khan.*

The pleasure peculiar to the romantic, as Coleridge conceived of it, is a reconciliation of the profound with the simple, the tragic with the marvelous, the serious with the humorous grotesque. The famous rejoinder to Mrs. Barbauld is to be understood as a definition of the genre:

As to the want of a moral, I told her that in my own judgment the poem had too much; and that the only, or chief fault, if I might say so, was the obtrusion of the moral sentiment so openly on the reader as a principle or cause of action in a work of such pure imagination. It ought to have had no more moral than the Arabian Nights' tale of the merchant's sitting down to eat dates by the side of a well, and throwing the shells aside, and lo! a genie starts up, and says he *must* kill the aforesaid merchant, because one of the date shells had, it seems, put out the eye of the genie's son.[13]

The romantic, as Coleridge was here expounding it, permits no explanations. To explain might inconveniently admit the judgment, in the role of a bull in a china shop. Everything must happen as it happens, with the apparent inevitability of dream, where the power of comparison is suspended—that state most friendly to illusion. Note that the genie "*must* kill the aforesaid merchant, *because* one of the date shells had, it seems, put out the eye of the genie's son"! The simulacrum of necessity is an organic part of the total effect of illusion.

It has been suggested that Coleridge was merely having Mrs. Barbauld on. He is also thought to have been saying that a work of pure imagination is so pure that it is meaningless.[14] In reality, however, his words constitute a keen professional analysis of the effect that is proper to the genre, and the means which are proper to secure it. Those words which should be emphasized especially are "*the obtrusion* of the moral sentiment *so openly* on the reader." The Arabian Nights analogy is a matter of immediate, not ultimate purpose, and does not exclude a metaphysical or moral meaning. Coleridge is saying simply that the romantic, like other poetry, is first of all art. A poem proposes "for its immediate object pleasure, not truth"; "and though truth, either moral or intellectual, ought to be the *ultimate* end, yet this will distinguish the character of the author, not the class to which the work belongs." The distinction between immediate and ultimate, between class and author, seems entirely clear, and adequate to reconcile the apparently divergent interests of truth and imaginative pleasure.

2

For Coleridge all imaginative writing depends upon the two principles of unity of interest, or proportionateness; and of sameness in difference. The romantic, the work of purest imagination, of all genres rests most heavily upon these principles: for in the romantic the element of difference from common sense reality is greatest, and likewise the skill which is required to make us accept this difference. "Each part [should be] proportionate, tho' the whole perhaps impossible."

"Difference in sameness"[15] is the reconciliation of opposites applied to artistic imitation. Unity is only intelligible in terms of oppositions, and these opposites cannot exist alone; each is essential to the other's existence. Likewise the imitation must differ from the thing imitated in order to reveal it: "all knowledge rests on the coincidence of an object with a subject."[16] Strangely a thing or unity is nothing in itself; we have no knowledge of it because we have no vantage point from which to view it. *The Ancient Mariner* imitates the unity of reality, the basic structure of human experience, the truths of religion and morality—but it presents the *truth* in a setting of literal impossibility.

Difference in sameness involves reconciliation between the opposite satisfactions of recognition and surprise. A disproportion between means and end is pleasurable, provided that it is apparently intentional and is ultimately resolved. This is the use of the ballad measure in *The Ancient Mariner*, which would seem too trivial for Coleridge's purposes. In this instance the pleasure comes from noticing the sameness before the difference, from mistaking the apparent naiveté of the metre for a naiveté in the poem, and from consequently being surprised to find more meaning than was bargained for. Expecting only the temperate pleasure which naturally accompanies a ballad, we are delighted by unhoped-for largesse, and pricked to unwonted attention.

Coleridge increases the pace of the ballad measure, and makes it a liquid flowing:

> The bride hath paced into the hall,
> Red as a rose is she;
> Nodding their heads before her goes
> The merry minstrelsy.

Occasionally he deviates into harshness, as the meaning demands it:

> It cracked and growled, and roared and howled,
> Like noises in a swound.

He increases intensity by widening the bounds which the ballad stanza imposes:

> We listened and looked sideways up!
> Fear at my heart, as at a cup,
> My life-blood seemed to sip!
> The stars were dim, and thick the night,
> The steerman's face by his lamp gleamed white;
> From the sails the dew did drip—
> Till clomb above the eastern bar
> The horned Moon, with one bright star
> Within the nether tip.

Thus the stanza can be deepened, can be rounded to a definite unit, with a beginning, a middle, and an end.

In *The Ancient Mariner* Coleridge brings ballad measure to maturity. (Its decadence can be profitably examined in *The Ballad of Reading Gaol*, which is to Coleridge as are Morris and Rossetti to *La Belle Dame Sans Merci*.) Coleridge modifies his pace with rich and copious rhyme and alliteration: the frequency of internal rhyme is a distinguishing mark of the poem. His pre-

Ancient Mariner are living by virtue of qualities which can be analyzed into personification, particularity, and selectivity.

The sun, the moon, the stars, the storm, are living, sentient beings, endowed with intelligence and will, and responsive to a central power beyond them:

The Sun came up upon the left,
Out of the sea came *he*!

And now the Storm-Blast came, and *he*
Was tyrannous and strong:
He struck with his o'ertaking wings,
And chased us south along.

The moving Moon went up the sky,
And nowhere did abide:
Softly *she* was going up,
And a star or two beside.
. . . .
The Sun's rim dips; the stars rush out:
At one stride comes the dark.

The principles of particularity and selectivity work together, in the touch which strikes the essential, and along with it the confident sparseness which convinces us that all is said. Thus the effectiveness of the water snakes, "Blue, glossy green, and velvet black," like the certainty of Keats in

And as I sat, over the *light blue* hills
There came a noise of revellers.[19]

The explicitly supernatural beings, "naturas invisibiles," contribute to the general aliveness of *The Ancient Mariner*. These beings are ranged in hierarchies, "thrones, principalities, and powers." The lonesome daemon of the Pole, the troop of spirits blest, the guardian saint of the Mariner ("Sure my kind saint took pity on me"), Mary Queen of Heaven, Christ, and God the Father

are the estates of spiritual power. The order and the fullness of
this supernatural kingdom correspond with Coleridge's general
sense of unity, which contains the notions of plenitude, variety,
degree, graduation, and modulation, fused in the imagination
of ideal life or spirit.

This hierarchy of the invisible has two effects upon the
meaning of *The Ancient Mariner*. First, it distinguishes the spirits
of nature from the Christian spirits. The daemon of the Pole,
"who bideth by himself / In the land of mist and snow," would
have strict justice from the Mariner, who has violated the order
of nature by shooting the albatross. This spirit yields reluctantly
to a higher power, which is merciful. Their relationship is that
of the ocean and the moon:

Still as a slave before his Lord,
The ocean hath no blast;
His great bright eye most silently
Up to the moon is cast—
If he may know which way to go;
For she guides him smooth or grim.
See, brother, see! how graciously
She looketh down on him.

Still more important is the effect of the hierarchy upon the
theme of the voyage. *The Ancient Mariner* is not the story of a
limitless quest; the Mariner is not Melville's Taji,[20] who vanishes in a boundless ocean. God, Christ, Mary, and the guardian
saint are associated with home, the church, and human society,
to which the Mariner returns with longing. True, he is fated to
"pass, like night, from land to land," but this is penance, not
choice. The argument is "how a Ship having passed the Line
was driven by storms to the cold Country towards the South
Pole." The sea voyage is certainly a part of *The Ancient Mariner*,
but its centrifugal urge is countered by an impulse which seeks
the center. As in Melville, though less elaborately, Coleridge
opposes the sea to the land, but unlike Melville's Bulkington, to
whom "in landlessness alone resides the highest truth,"[21] the

Mariner seeks the haven of the harbor-bay, in which alone is light, firmness, and truth.

The rock shone bright, the kirk no less,
That stands above the rock:
The moonlight steeped in silentness
The steady weathercock.

Imagery of the land structurally foreshadows the Mariner's spiritual redemption:

Sometimes a-dropping from the sky
I heard the sky-lark sing.
. . . .
. . . yet still the sails made on
A pleasant noise till noon,
A noise like of a hidden brook
In the leafy month of June.
. . . .
It raised my hair, it fanned my cheek
Like a meadow-gale of spring—
It mingled strangely with my fears.
Yet it felt like a welcoming.

Undoubtedly the sea voyage stands for a spiritual adventure, as E. M. W. Tillyard has said. "The Mariner and his voyage signify the mental adventure of an unusually inquiring spirit."[22] The narrative is rounded, with a beginning, a middle, and an end, whereas in the pure quest for an infinite goal there can obviously be no genuine end. If anything *The Ancient Mariner* comes closer to having no beginning, in keeping with its genre. The initial improbability has to be overleaped, the ties with common reality immediately cut. Coleridge plunges in medias res with breathtaking speed, which is significantly a characteristic of the entire poem—the ship reaches the South Pole in eight stanzas, including two intermissions for the Wedding Guest to beat his breast.

The Pole is a region of terror and chaos, faintly touched with beauty in ice "green as emerald." Polar, it is a place of extremes, of absolute isolation, in which the human mind cannot long survive. It is a kind of insanity, based on a delirium.

The ice was here, the ice was there,
The ice was all around:
It cracked and growled, and roared and howled,
Like noises in a swound!

The coming of the Albatross revives the mind's normal association; the sailors hail it "as if it had been a Christian soul." It frees the ship from polar isolation.

The ice did split with a thunder-fit;
The helmsman steered us through!

But the Mariner wantonly kills the albatross, the emissary of life. The crime is a failure of imagination, a negation of the living spirit. It breaks the chain of being, upon whose continuity depends the living oneness of organic unity. It is irrational and inexplicable as all evil is from one point of view inexplicable, an aberration from the norm. Its mere frivolity is the most striking thing about it, a causeless impulse from a spiritual void.

The calm which soon follows upon the dead is the counterpart of polar isolation, an abnormal state of mind. This equatorial calm is likewise an extreme, and the "extremes meet" in identical isolation and immobility. As it was previously icebound, so now the ship seems riveted in its place by the baleful eye of the sun. In Coleridge calm is often evil, as in *Dejection: An Ode*, in which mental suffering is exacerbated by its very passivity:

A grief without a pang, void, dark, and drear,
Which finds no natural outlet, no relief,
In word, or sigh, or tear.

The calm on the Pacific Line is a natural consequence of the crime; it is the nadir of the fallen mind. But total passivity is impossible. If health has ceased, disease must take its place. Thus the rotting of the sea, the monstrous creatures of the calm, the phosphorescence of decay:

About, about, in reel and rout
The death-fires danced at night;
The water, like a witch's oils,
Burnt green, and blue and white.

The drouth too is a natural symbol for mental impotence:

And every tongue, through utter drought,
Was withered at the root.

We recall that the Mariner is forced to drink his own blood in order to achieve utterance: "at a dear ransom he freeth his speech from the bonds of thirst," says the gloss. And the eventual breaking of the spell is represented, in a familiar romantic metaphor, by the gushing of a spring within the heart: an inner movement figured outwardly in the rain which follows.

Wind in *The Ancient Mariner* is catastrophic in the storm, but afterwards entirely beneficent.[23] It is at first mere necessary accident, but becomes a symbol for mind, or mental action. The aspects and movements of nature in *The Ancient Mariner* are, as has been said, alive. They are perhaps most simply accounted for as unusual in order to excite wonder; and swift, abrupt, and various in order to achieve surprise. These latter are requirements of the genre, and need not preclude more searching explorations. Such effects are reinforced by the syntax, which notably avoids logical relationships, confining itself to *and* connections of addition and sequence. Logic, since it tries to explain, is presumably the antithesis of wonder.[24]

The Ancient Mariner is a tale of crime, punishment, and redemption,[25] in a unified world of interrelationships,[26] cemented by imaginative sympathy and love. The Mariner's deed is a sin against imagination, an action which symbolically destroys the principle of life and order. It comes from insensitiveness, negation, passivity, and not from any positive motive. The consequences of the deed are represented in the calm, and in the terrible isolation of "life-in-death." The Mariner commences his redemption when he achieves the state of mind which it is the purpose of the poem to inculcate; when he can see truth as beauty, or see the beauty of the real. The water snakes, which in his fallen state have seemed hideous and despicable, "a thousand thousand slimy things," are now happy things of inexpressible beauty, which he blesses. Beauty, then, is a pathway to spiritual truth and redemption.[27]

4

The Romantic Unity of *Kubla Khan*

In his valuable book *Keats' Craftsmanship*, M. R. Ridley has cited
Kubla Khan along with the "magic casements" passage of Keats's
Nightingale ode as the very essence of "the distilled sorceries of
Romanticism," and his statement is more or less typical. This
concept of "romantic magic" has its sanction and is by no means
to be discarded as pointless. In practice, however, it has had the
unfortunate effect of discouraging critical analysis; and it likewise plays into the hands of those of our contemporaries who
incline to look upon romantic poetry as a kind of moonlit mist,
which dissolves at the touch of reality and reason.

The fascinating but uncritical study of Lowes, with its emphasis upon the irrational and the unconscious, and its untiring
quest for sources, has had an equally unfortunate and discouraging influence. Only with the work of Elisabeth Schneider and
others who have pointed the way, has it become possible to think
of *Kubla Khan* as other than a kind of magnificent freak and to
treat it as an intelligible poem which lies open to critical exami-

nation. And the influence of Lowes still imposes upon the student the tyranny of source study. He has opened so wide a field for speculation that scholars are still inclined rather to revise or enlarge his conclusions than to proceed to the task of the critic.

The study of possible sources for Coleridge's imagery is valuable. Whatever we can get, in fact, in the way of information on the genesis and the circumstances of a poem is useful. Such information, however, can be dangerous if we exaggerate its function and substitute it for the poem itself. It is background, not foreground. To discover, for instance, a parallel between a passage in Plato and a poem of Coleridge is valuable when it adds to the poem's potential meaning; but the discovery is misused if Plato is permitted to determine what Coleridge is talking about. The proper place to study Coleridge's poetry is ultimately *The Poetical Works of Samuel Taylor Coleridge*.

By implication the foregoing incautious remarks bind this essay to a twofold effort: first, to give such an account of *Kubla Khan*'s "distilled sorceries" and "romantic magic" as will reconcile them with the rational and discursive processes of criticism; and, second, to account for them within the bounds of the poem. As to the first, no one need fear that our romantic magic will be dispelled, such a pyrrhic victory as that lying quite beyond either the powers or the wishes of the present writer. As to the second, I hope for a generously loose construction as to what the bounds of the poem include.

A number of contentions must precede the specific examination of *Kubla Khan*. First, the immediate literary effect intended and obtained in it by Coleridge is pleasure—a pleasure which derives from that very romantic sorcery of which we have spoken. This pleasure, as Pope says of nature, is "the source, and end, and test" of poetic art. It is not necessary, of course, to claim that Coleridge has found the only means of attaining it. Second, this pleasure is in no way incompatible with even the profoundest meaning; is in fact inseparable from meaning. The basic criterion for poetry is in the broadest sense human interest: a poem should deal with a human situation of universal interest treated with sympathy, judgment, and insight. This human significance is not to be regarded as a monopoly of the classical or neoclassical humanist but belongs to the romantic poet as well. Third, *Kubla Khan* embodies the Coleridgean doctrine of "the reconciliation of opposites." On this point be it added that the authority of the poem is at least equal to prose definitions of these doctrines; it is the living word, as opposed to the skeleton of abstract definition. Neither, however, is fully intelligible without the other. Finally, *Kubla Khan* is in the most essential sense a completed work, in that it symbolizes and comprehends the basic romantic dilemma, a crucial problem of art.

To avoid misunderstanding, let us preface interpretation of the poem with a self-evident but necessary distinction. *Kubla Khan* is "fanciful" rather than "realistic"; the simplest, most basic pleasure it provides stems rather from its distance from actuality than from any verisimilitude or skillful imitation of matter of fact. It belongs in the category of what Dryden called "the fairy way of poetry," and consideration of its meaning must be controlled by our understanding of this limitation. With this conceded, however, we can still demonstrate the immensely important fact of its basic humanity and significance. The setting of *Kubla Khan* is pleasurable and well removed from any contact with the sharp edges of the actual; yet within its enchanted garden we shall find problems of the weightiest import. Thus the central situation of the poem is the spacious pleasure-garden of Kubla:

So twice five miles of fertile ground
With walls and towers were girdled round.

And the poem itself is embodied in this garden, various, extensive, yet inclosed from the world without. But our estimate of the situation is incomplete if it ignores the implications of the towered walls. A reality against which we must fortify ourselves is hardly a reality which we can ignore. We must then extend our definition to include this implication and consider the core of the poem to reside in an opposition or stress between the garden, artificial and finite, and the indefinite, inchoate, and possibly turbulent outside world.

Since, however, what lies beyond the walls is only implied, not imaged, we must pass to whatever relationships exist inside them.

In Xanadu did Kubla Khan
A stately pleasure-dome decree.

This pleasure-dome is the focal point of the physical setting and is correspondingly important. Within the bounds of the encircled garden, the pleasure-dome and the river are the opposites to be reconciled. The pleasure-dome is associated with man, as Kubla is an emblem of man; it figures his desire for pleasure and safety; it stands for strictly human and finite values. The image of the dome suggests agreeable sensations of roundedness and smoothness; the creation of man, its quasi-geometrical shape is simpler than the forms of nature which surround it, yet blends with them. This dome, however, also evokes the religious—it is in some sort a temple, if only to the mere mortal Kubla Khan. And thus there is also a blending or interfusion with its opposite, the sacred river Alph.

The pleasure-dome is the chosen refuge of Kubla the mighty, the emperor whose every whim is law, who would have temptations toward hubris. It is the center of his retreat in his haughty withdrawal from a world unworthy of him. It is above and beyond nature, a "miracle of rare device" in which man transcends and circumvents mere natural processes. It stands amid an enormous garden in which a considerable segment of wild nature is isolated and imprisoned for the delight of the human Kubla.

And there were gardens bright with sinuous rills,
Where blossomed many an incense-bearing tree;

And here were forests ancient as the hills,
Enfolding sunny spots of greenery.

This description hints, however, that nature here is an uneasy prisoner, or perhaps a prisoner who is bounded only during
her own pleasure. The "forests ancient" suggest an existence
unknown to man and uncoerced by human power, whose sway
over it is temporary and precarious. It is a force and being
unlike man, busy about its own purposes and, like the serpent,
inscrutable in the labyrinthine wanderings of the "sinuous rills"
of the gardens.

Here one may affirm that this setting illustrates a typical
romantic conception of "the reconciliation of opposites" by
means of a concrete, visual scene. By a process of shading and
gradation in light and dark, in garden and forest, oppositions
become blended, interfused, and unified; and this visual unification extends to the feelings and ideas which the scene evokes.
This is the romantic "picturesque," more fully to be seen in the
landscape of Wordsworth's *Lines . . . above Tintern Abbey*, with its
complex blending of sky and valley, of man and nature, objectified in blending and gradation of color and form. In *Kubla Khan*
the effect permits us simultaneously and with no sense of paradox or jar to receive the gardens as the elaborate plaything of
a great potentate, the emblem of his pride, exclusiveness, and
power, and also as an ironic commentary upon the impossibility
of any real ownership of nature.

These oppositions, however, are only a subtheme or prelude.
The river is the true exemplar of nonhuman forces, subhuman
and superhuman alike. Even the "deep romantic chasm" of its
rising is incompatible with the order of Kubla's pleasure-
grounds. It "slants athwart"; it cuts across the pattern. The
simile of the "woman wailing for her demon-lover" invests it
with the supernatural, the *Arabian Nights* wonder and fear of the
jinni, beings unfriendly to man and yet obscurely connected
with him.

Of the river itself most noticeable is the brevity of its surface course in relation to the hidden potentialities of its subterranean flowing:

Five miles meandering with a mazy motion
Through wood and dale the sacred river ran,
Then reached the caverns measureless to man
And sank in tumult to a lifeless ocean.

Treated as a whole and in its relationship with the dome and the pleasure-grounds, the river is the primordial and the irrational, whatever lies beyond the control of the rational and conscious mind. The power of the source, vividly imaged in the dancing rocks—

And from this chasm, with ceaseless turmoil seething
As if this earth in fast thick pants were breathing,
A mighty fountain momently was forced
Amid whose swift half-intermitted burst
Huge fragments vaulted like rebounding hail,
Or chaffy grain beneath the thresher's flail:
And 'mid these dancing rocks at once and ever
It flung up momently the sacred river . . . —

is a power beyond mortal man, even beyond Kubla Khan. This source is creation and birth, a force and urge at once frenetic and turbulent and also rhythmical and regular. At the mouth is death, icy and lifeless, where Alph in tumult returns to the underground. As with the source, powers unknown and uncontrollable are at work, descending at last to quiescence. Here are potentialities not of death absolutely but relative to what can be imagined and experienced.

Thus the opposition between river and dome. But here we must shift our emphasis, as previously with the pleasure-grounds themselves, more fully to Alph. The river is human life, past, present, and future, birth, life, and death. For five miles it runs upon the surface, consents, "meandering with a mazy motion," to harmonize with the order of Kubla's estate, to yield to his power. It is like Bede's famous bird that flies in a moment through the warm hall, swiftly proceeding from unknown birth to unknown death. And Kubla in his pleasure-dome is man, living in his special cosmos of palace and garden, but hearing "the mingled measure / From the fountain and the caves." Impulses unaccountable, creative and deadly alike, comprehending more of life than the reason can grasp. It is amid the tumult that Kubla hears the ominous prophecy of war, and this from the dying, the caves of ice. The poem as narrative can go no further than this, for the destruction is implied of Kubla's elaborate and artificial escape. The complex order and equilibrium of his existence are overset by the mere hint. This statement implies, of course, that the pattern must not within the poem be broken and that Kubla is never to emerge from his walled pleasure-grounds.

Yet in an important sense the pattern *is* broken in that Coleridge continues the lyric but abandons the story. Suddenly the imagery shifts to the "damsel with a dulcimer." This damsel, the Abyssinian maid, is most simply comparable to the muse invoked by the classical poet. She has, as has been suggested, a relation to Milton's heavenly muse Urania, as the stimulating speculations about the source of "Mount Abora" indicate. It is valuable to compare her also, as does Miss Schneider, to Platonic inspiration, the *furor poeticus* of the bard. Appropriately, however, to Coleridge's romanticism and to the special context of *Kubla Khan*, she is wild and remote, with the glamour and terror of a far-off, mysterious land, marvelous, inaccessible, yet rich with the significant associations of literature. So Keats in a lyric much akin to *Kubla Khan*:

I saw parched Abyssinia rouse and sing
To the silver cymbals' ring!
I saw the whelming vintage hotly pierce
Old Tartary the fierce!—

The damsel is as well the ideal singer, the archetypal poet. The transmission of her song, if transmission there could be, would be like the conception of imitation in Longinus, where the divine fire passes from poet to poet, and Plato emulates Homer in the beneficent rivalry of genius. But Coleridge is modest, with the clear sense that the song can never be equaled:

Could I revive within me
Her symphony and song,
To such a deep delight 'twould win me
That with music loud and long
I would build that dome in air.

The phrase "deep delight" carries us into the problem of pleasure, more especially into the problem of the pleasure which the particular poem *Kubla Khan* should provide. This delight is for Coleridge as well as Wordsworth the prerequisite of poetic creation, the imaginative joy and effluence described in *Dejection: An Ode*. But here it is also an effect peculiar to the poem itself: a kind of magic, an apparently naive delight in the presentation of wonders, and in gorgeous images evoked in imagination in the sort of pleasure suggested by the classic ancient accounts of Plato, Aristotle, and Longinus.

This pleasure is also partly from variety and fulness—wonders which satisfy, as for a child at a carnival. These qualities are embodied not only in the imagery but in fulness and variety of melodic movement in the verse, which would bear more thorough discussion than can be given here. The word "symphony" in line 43 is not lightly or carelessly used. The delight is rounded and completed by the dark tinge of the "deep romantic chasm," the turbulent power of the river, the doom of the ancestral voices, and lastly by the mingling of dread and enchantment in the closing lines, where the holiness of the inspired poet is in a sense unholy too, an affair as it were of the infernal gods as much as the clear deity of Apollo.

The interpretation in earlier pages has attempted to demonstrate an essential profundity and universality in the theme of *Kubla Khan*. It remains to assert that pleasure is in no way incompatible with significance. In some contemporary poetry and criticism there seems implicit the notion that it is somehow dishonest and shameful to please, an attitude which has tellingly been termed "the new Puritanism." One feels inclined to renew the old question, "Dost thou think, because thou art virtuous, there shall be no more cakes and ale?" But in *Kubla Khan*, as probably in all good romantic poetry, the pleasure which draws us within the poem is also inseparable from its full meaning. Imaginative delight in the wonders of the pleasure-ground is indispensable to the sense of their opposite. Fully to appreciate the theme's potentialities, we must be beguiled into believing momentarily in the permanency of the impermanent, the possibility of the impossible. The fullest meaning, a synthesis of antitheses, calls for feeling and imagination at full stretch, reconciled with intellectual scope and understanding. And pleasure, one may claim, is the basis and beginning of the process.

Our final contention reemphasizes the depth and significance of *Kubla Khan*. It is in the truest sense a completed work, in that it symbolizes and comprehends the crucial romantic dilemma. In a more obvious sense it is clearly unfinished: as a narrative it barely commences, and it shifts abruptly with the Abyssinian maid from objective to subjective. Considered as lyric, however, it is self-contained and whole. The romantic poet as idealist and monist strives to include within his cosmos both actual and ideal, as in Coleridge, Wordsworth, Shelley, even Byron, and to some extent Keats. His attempt, however, coexists with his consciousness that he seeks the unattainable; the ideal can never be fully actualized. Thus in good romantic poetry there is a continuous tension, compacted of the sense of the immense potentialities of his theme set off against the knowledge that they can only partially be realized. This tension and conflict can be reconciled and rendered valuable partly by the poet's own belief in the value of the attempt itself. The poet excels himself as it were by force; he is stimulated to creation rather than falling into despair. Above all he benefits by understanding and accepting his dilemma even while trying to rise above it nonetheless.

And this is eminently the case with *Kubla Khan*. Coleridge

provides a scene and experience too fine for common nature's daily food. With exquisite judgment he forbears the attempt to explain what can only be hinted and dramatizes instead what is lost in the very fact of relinquishing it. But amid the master-artist's skillful manipulation of interest and suspense, his suggestions of "more than meets the eye," is the human interest, the complexity and spacious grasp, without which the rest would be nothing, could not separately exist. Properly understood, romantic poetry is never a cheat, although it often labors under the disadvantage of being extremely agreeable.

5

The Dejection of Coleridge's Ode

Coleridge's *Dejection: An Ode* is not quite so gloomy as the title would suggest, and as students of the poem have generally maintained. This conclusion is in one sense revolutionary; in another, as I hope to show, it is natural and inevitable to the verge of the obvious.

It is usually assumed that the dejection of the *Ode* is both deep and unrelieved—melancholy at its most atrabilious. Fred Manning Smith, in an article examining its relation to Wordsworth's *Intimations*, remarks that "in Wordsworth's *Ode* grief finds relief and ends in joy; in Coleridge's, grief finds no relief and ends in dejection."[1] Elisabeth Schneider in her excellent treatment of *Kubla Khan* has likewise employed it as a touchstone for gloom: "The dejection [of *Kubla Khan*] is not deep and hopeless as in the ode."[2]

Both of these statements are, of course, true in their contexts, but they are both inadequate, just as they are both typical. They are epitomes of the accepted view of the *Ode*. This view has arisen and remained unchallenged probably because *Dejection* has hardly been studied as a poem at all; its enormous biographical and philosophical importance has obscured its poetic structure. It has been treated as a reflection of irretrievable personal disaster, as a lament for Coleridge's impending loss of poetic imagination, and as the expression of a despairing subjectivism; but seldom as a poetic object and unity.

Thus de Sélincourt has correlated the *Ode* with Coleridge's life. By establishing and publishing its earliest version he is able to draw valuable biographical conclusions—that the *Ode* was originally addressed to Sara Hutchinson, rather than to Wordsworth; that it arises directly from the circumstances of Coleridge's hopeless marriage and his equally hopeless love of Sarah; and that it signalizes his approaching loss of poetic power, as a direct result of these insuperable domestic and amatory difficulties.[3]

The philosophical or metaphysical interpretation of *Dejection*, which develops naturally from the biographical view, utilizes a single passage (ll. 45–58) to point out the *Ode*'s unhappy subjectivism. This passage, "O lady! we receive but what we give," is for the philosophical approach the core of the poem, expressing as it does a crisis in Coleridge's thinking about the relationship of nature and the mind—a disturbance of the subject-object balance which he sought to maintain in both philosophy and poetry.[4]

Each of these approaches is entirely valid in its own sphere, and is indeed indispensable as a preliminary to a full and accurate reading of the poem. But let us not confuse our purposes. If we attempt to substitute biography, or philosophy, for the poem itself, we shall be using methods inappropriate to the end to be attained, and are likely to find ourselves possessed of unsatisfactory conclusions: unsatisfactory not because untrue, but because they are half-true, incomplete, and misleading. Taken as a literary structure the *Ode* in its wholeness is more interesting and more valuable than an abstract proposition drawn from a part of it only: as Coleridge himself warns, "that which suits a part infects the whole." Taken as an "imitation" of the mind which made it, as Coleridge would take it,[5] it expresses a richer, more varied, fuller experience than the sense of flat defeat to which the biographical approach must bring us, or the static rigor of the philosophical conclusion.

In attempting to describe the *Ode*'s evolving meaning, I shall assume the authority of the established text of 1817 as its most perfect version, and shall assume also that Coleridge as a metaphysical realist[6] and a romantic poet of nature is expressing his experience through the interaction of his thoughts and emotions with natural symbolism and imagery. Whether or not this relationship is harmonious, the objectification of the mind by means of external nature is the only method available to him in this poem. Consequently considerable stress will be placed on what may be termed "the natural situation," as it develops over a period of hours; with the interaction of the wind and the aeolian harp (a crystallizing symbol of mind and nature), the significance of the moon, and the objectification of the various shifts and developments of mood by means of the rising and changing wind. This relationship, however, is "symbolic" rather than "allegorical." These equivalences of mind and nature are suggested, not explicit; they are dynamic and variable, not fixed and exact. They may be characterized by Coleridge's own conception of symbol as "that which means what it says and something more besides";[7] thus the natural setting of the *Ode* is objectively present, not the mere servant of allegory—but it is also the medium of Coleridge's meaning.

In strophe 1 the "natural situation" is a tranquil night, amid which light winds "mould yon cloud in lazy flakes," and cause a

... dull sobbing draft, that moans and
   rakes
Upon the strings of this Aeolian lute,
Which better far were mute.

                                  (ll. 6 – 8)

The phenomenon of the new moon with the old moon in her lap, however, forewarns of storm to come. The tone and the particulars of the moon image, one may suggest, are themselves in no way ominous, but rounded and agreeable, with the hint of that same effluence of light which later on in the poem is used to symbolize joy (ll. 9–12).[8] Strophe 2 describes Coleridge's mood at its nadir of dejection:

A grief without a pang, void, dark, and drear,
A stifled, drowsy, unimpassioned grief,
Which finds no natural outlet, no relief
   In word, or sigh, or tear.

(ll. 20–24)

This state of mind is the counterpart of the natural setting of strophe 1, which objectifies it in the light wind, the lazy cloud, and the sobbing draft, inharmonious yet dull and passive. The aeolian harp "had better far be mute" because at present it expresses only discord. The moon phenomenon is a harbinger not of disaster but of hope, for only a storm will clear the air, and only some violence of release will rescue Coleridge from the prison house of his dejection. The relationship between nature and mind is explicitly stated in ll. 15–20, in which Coleridge prays for the wind and the rain that "Might startle this dull pain, and make it move and live." The way is prepared, then, for a natural cycle which shall move from calm to storm to calm again, the last as it were a reconciliation; and Coleridge's own statement in strophe 1 warrants us in interpreting the development of his mood according to the same design.

Strophe 2, after setting forth his dejection, states his peculiar dilemma—of the beautiful forms of nature he must say only

I see them all so excellently fair,
I see, not feel, how beautiful they are!

(ll. 37–38)

Only through joy, he continues, can we have more

Than that inanimate cold world allowed
To the poor loveless ever-anxious crowd.

(ll. 51–52)

Our world is created by ourselves, and only the power of joy can endow it with life and meaning. This power of joy,[9] essential to the poet, Coleridge has now lost, robbed of it by repeated afflictions, and with it (I should be inclined to say in this poem identical with it) his "shaping spirit of imagination." Joy and imagination, it should be noticed, are active agencies, by which the mind creates, shapes, and unifies its vision of reality; dejection is passive and inert, uncreative and lifeless.

The poet's griefs rise to their climax in strophe 6. In combatting them his "sole resource" has been "to be still and patient all I can"—to deaden his nature (see ll. 89–90) by "abstruse research." This ill-advised attempt more even than the afflictions which caused it to be made has *nullified* the creative imagination, for he has sought to suppress the very activity which made creation possible. Understanding, the abstracting and calculative power, he has cultivated; but understanding alone leaves the world essentially dead, inert, and inorganic.[10] Coleridge has committed the very sin which he most fears against himself; he has mutilated the living organism of mind, destroyed its complex harmonies, upset its ordered hierarchy by seeking to substitute a part for the whole.[11]

Now, to return to the natural setting, as Coleridge does in the following strophe 7, this unhappy self-mutilation has been brought about by a deliberate passivity, for the "abstruse research" which has so disproportionately exercised the understanding was undertaken to deaden, not to arouse, the spirit; and sluggishly rules its scattered kingdom in default of the banished creative power. This passivity, this "stillness" and "patience," is equivalent to the oppressive calm of nature in strophe 1. The logic of the relationship, in company with the storm warning of the new moon (ll. 9–14), demands that this stagnant spell be broken, and declares that any change which involves activity must be a change for the better. And accordingly at the beginning of strophe 7 Coleridge rouses from his melancholy introspection to find that the wind has risen, and the storm is at its full.

The aeolian lute, earlier touched only by a "dull sobbing draft" (ll. 6–7), now screams as if in agony (ll. 97–98). The wind, a "Mad Lutanist," raves among the leaves and blossoms, becomes a tragic actor; and then a mighty epic poet who sings of a host in rout, of groans and of tramplings (ll. 104–113). Action disorganized and painful, but action nonetheless, and as such clearly preferable to the earlier deathlike lull. The feelings are awake, the imagination, though imperfectly, is at work. Storm follows calm, strife has supplanted uneasy peace, as in a plot at the height of its complication, and after a moment of rest comes the reconciliation or denouement.

> . . . all that noise, as of a rushing crowd,
> With groans, and tremulous shudderings—all is over—
> It tells another tale, with sounds less deep and loud!
>   *A tale of less affright*
>   *And tempered with delight* [italics mine],
> As Otway's self had framed the tender lay.
>
>   (ll. 115–120)

These lines express a further development of the imagination, a more complex organization in which the shaping power moulds into unity the diverse elements of grief, fear, and their opposite delight (see l. 124). Strife, in effect, has given way to reconciliation, and for Coleridge only the imagination can reconcile. The mind, recalled to activity, has regained its wholeness. Ceasing to flee, it has faced its difficulties and in part at least has overcome them.

In the final strophe, in which the poem is symbolically brought by midnight to a term, Coleridge returns to the "Dear

Lady" to whom the poem is addressed. He wishes her a gentle sleep, and prays that

... this storm be but a mountain-birth,
May all the stars hang bright above her dwelling,
　Silent as though they watched the sleeping Earth!

(ll. 129–131)

Here, I believe, two points are to be noticed. First is the significance of Coleridge's turning here to another: that he is able to wish her well, to forget himself in imagination of the peace and joy which he invokes in her behalf and of the creative vision of reality (ll. 135–136), the ability "to see into the life of things," which only joy can give. This argues for the rebirth of his imagination, which in Coleridge as in Wordsworth, Shelley, and Keats is the faculty which enables us to escape the prison of self and participate in other lives and modes of being.[12] The second point, interesting though less material, is that Coleridge wishes for his friend peace and clear skies untouched by disturbance. Having in the poem imaginatively portrayed a hard won balance attained only by struggle, for another he asks a simpler, more static equilibrium. The implications give food for thought.

Examination of *Dejection: An Ode*, then, reveals a more highly organized, a more rounded, and comprehensive experience than investigation of either its biographical or its philosophical elements can uncover. Having stated a truth, however, let us not do a disservice by exaggerating it, or by confusing our purposes. The reconciliation achieved in the *Ode* is relative, not absolute, just as common sense will tell us that Coleridge's dejection could not be absolute, nor his difficulties wholly crushing. There is no disposition here to deny that these difficulties were great, nor that his poetic powers were, as he says, permanently impaired. What is affirmed basically is that the poem itself will yield us more valuable, subtler, and truer insights than any nonliterary abstraction from it can attain.

6

The Imaginal Design of Shelley's
Ode to the West Wind

Such an exposition as I am about to attempt requires some
justification, especially when the poem to be expounded is almost universally known, widely recognized as a masterpiece,
and reprinted in hundreds of anthologies of English poetry.
Only a few years ago this enterprise would have been reckoned
quite unnecessary. Today, however, the situation is somewhat
changed. The gentle—or ungentle—art of explication is enjoying a still increasing vogue, while at the same time our most
influential explicators have been categorically, and to me un-
warrantably, hostile to Shelley. John Crowe Ransom considers
him merely feeble, Allen Tate indicts him for confusion of metaphor—a terrible charge in contemporary criticism, despite the
immortal evidence of the "To be or not to be" soliloquy—and
Cleanth Brooks in *Modern Poetry and the Tradition* consigns him to
limbo posthaste as "a very unsatisfactory poet," sentimental and
guilty of "poor craftsmanship." Those, on the other hand, who
know Shelley best have generally been too much occupied with

learning still more about him to heed the attackers, who are frequently, as in the instances I have cited, critics of unquestionable influence and power. A detailed defense, as this is intended to be, of a lyric generally accepted as representative of Shelley at his best, should therefore fill a genuine need.

The general standards employed here, I am confident, would be approved even by Shelley's most uncompromising disapprovers, being, in fact, their own; although it might be remarked that they used to belong to Samuel Taylor Coleridge. Broadly I assume that a good poem should impose an imaginative unity upon diverse materials; that it should provide a complex human problem with a satisfactory solution; that through the medium of artistic form it should give coherence to the intellectual, emotional, and sensuous experience of the poet.

My method, however, is unlike theirs in being deliberately tentative, eclectic, and impure. Undoubtedly the poem itself is the important issue, but despite much contemporary opinion it should not be isolated from the mind of the poet, his environment, his artistic theories, and the body of his poetry. To do so, in my opinion, is to deprive the poem of its legitimate background, leaving only general criteria which can too easily be manipulated to serve the prejudices of the critic. It is interesting, by the way, that those who are austerest in approaching romantic poetry are often less abstemious in other situations. Cleanth Brooks, for example, advances upon Shelley equipped only with his standards and his bare fists. He has, however, given us excellent expositions of the esoteric background of Eliot's *The Waste Land* and of the eccentric historico-cosmogony of Yeats, with no apparent feeling that these are irrelevant.

No explication, fortunately, can entirely account for a poem. One may dilute, expand, and appreciate, but full explanation is impossible. Interpretation, I believe, must be tentative, and frankly metaphorical. Some method must obviously be found, and some standard of judgment applied, but no method or standard dare claim unique validity. I shall attempt to define what I see in the poem in its own particularity, rather than, as has become the predominant practice, what I do not see. My standards, save in the general sense, which has earlier been specified, derive from the poem itself, and I introduce whatever material seems calculated to advance understanding and appreciation of it. In order to speak fully of the imagery, which is perhaps most vital, I am regretfully compelled to omit consideration of the stanzaic, rhetorical, syntactical, and sound patterns, although these are well worthy of thorough study. Finally, my immediate purpose is to demonstrate that the *Ode to the West Wind* is a lyric of great complexity and consummate artistic design.

On the most elementary level, the poem deals in the first three stanzas with the action of the West Wind upon the leaf, the cloud, and the wave. Through this action Shelley steps progressively toward an imaginative examination of the possibility of identifying himself with the wind, and what it stands for. These first three stanzas are, at any rate on the surface, objective descriptions of natural phenomena. In stanza 4 the identification is suggested, tentatively and provisionally, through nature, in terms which bind the natural pattern of leaf-cloud-wave firmly to the emerging personality of the poet:

If I were a dead leaf thou mightest bear;
If I were a swift cloud to fly with thee;
A wave to pant beneath thy power.

and culminates in stanza 5—"Be thou, Spirit fierce, My spirit! Be thou me, impetuous one!"

This identification represents, so to speak, the unity which the poem is to win from variety. The individual is to be merged with the general; Shelley is to become the instrument through which speaks the universal voice. The medium by which this unity is imaginatively achieved is the nature-imagery of the three beginning stanzas—the action upon and the interrelationship of the West Wind with the leaf, the cloud, and the wave.

The stress, or structure, or problem of the *Ode* may also be defined as the death and regeneration contrast, which has been discussed by I. J. Kapstein, Newman Ivey White, and others. For the West Wind is both destroyer and preserver; it shatters established structures that new ones may be built from their ruins; it scatters the withered leaves, but in order to "quicken a new birth." This contrast, like the individual-general contrast earlier mentioned, needs and gets a poetic reconciliation, a unification concretely and emotionally satisfying.

This theme is partially developed in stanza 1, in which the wind scatters and disperses the forms of nature, but preserves its order and continuity by spreading the "winged seeds" where at the propitious time they may issue forth anew. Stanza 1, we may add, has a dual function or design. It introduces the contrast of death and rebirth, autumn and spring, but it also serves to introduce the leaf-image of the leaf-cloud-wave pattern. Here we must notice a difficulty in our terms. Reference to the death and regeneration theme is likely to be misleading unless we point out that the West Wind of Autumn, while both destroyer and preserver, is not also regenerator. The difference is more than a technicality, for it will fundamentally affect our notion of what Shelley is writing about: what he claims for the wind and for his own poetry.

It is left for another West Wind, the Zephyrus or Favonius of Horace and Virgil, "thine azure sister of the Spring," to blow "her clarion o'er the dreaming earth," and recall to life the dead who do but sleep. The West Wind of Autumn is a power of destruction, which nevertheless preserves whatever of the existing order is vital and promising. Fruition, however, is left to another power, kindred but still distinct. Shelley, in fact, is more modest, even amidst affirmation, than would appear at a glance. Indeed, it might be pointed out that not merely here but even in the earlier and less mature *Revolt of Islam* (9. 21–24) the same personal modesty tempers revolutionary confidence and hope.

Predominant, then, is the expression of a dynamic force, the tremendous power of revolutionary change. In stanza 2 the wind is both architect and wrecker of "the approaching storm," whose "congregated might of vapors" will give vent to the bursting forth of "black rain, and fire, and hail." The mingled menace, power, and beauty of the clouds, agents of the unseen wind, are symbolized in complex personifications: "*Angels* of rain and lightning," and the "*bright hair* uplifted from the head of some *fierce Maenad.*" Images of height and motion artfully contribute to the attraction—and repulsion—aroused by the scene: "the *steep* sky's *commotion* (a richly synthetic term); "even from the dim verge of the horizon to the Zenith's height": along with the motor and kinesthetic force of "loose clouds . . . *shed* "; "*shook* from the tangled boughs . . . "; "black rain . . . will burst." The scene is full of movement and force, applied to the solid structure of the "vaulted dome" of the sky. The suggestion that the change may be beneficent and fruitful is subtly implied by the linking of the clouds to the "decaying leaves" of stanza 1, carried further in the "*tangled boughs* of Heaven and Ocean," with their connotations of cyclical and reciprocal interfertilization.

In stanza 2 Shelley has viewed the revolutionary process complexly, as at once beautiful and terrible, fruitful and destructive; and he has reconciled these opposites, has unified and given them form, by the widely inclusive picture of wind, storm, and sky, simultaneously visible and harmoniously interrelated. In stanza 3 another difficulty is to be met and conquered.

Change and reform, in their iconoclastic vigor, destroy good as well as evil, for in the fabric of society the two are inextricably interwoven. The exquisite calm of the blue Mediterranean must be rudely shattered, although it frames in its motionless and idealizing medium ("the wave's intenser day") the loveliest forms of the past. The mellow patina of the centuries has its own attractions. We must also consider that the scene is Baiae, with its mingled associations of social splendor, amenity, and injustice. These "old palaces and towers," spiritualized by their medium (itself an emblem of the perspective of time), and softened by their clothing of time and nature, are almost overpowering to sensibility: "so sweet the sense faints picturing them."

If it is suspected that I am overreading these lines, I would refer the doubter to Shelley's *Philosophical View of Reform*, in which he takes account in explicit and abstract prose of the

problem here expressed poetically and imaginally. "Tyranny,"
he remarks among other things, "entrenches itself within the
existing interests of the best and most refined citizens of a nation
and says 'If you dare trample upon these, be free.' " Or note the
subtly blended delight and reprehension projected in the *Lines
Written Among the Euganean Hills*, as the poet looks down at the
"column, tower, and dome, and spire" of beautiful and dishon-
ored Venice. Or examine in *Adonais* the atmosphere of lovely,
decadent Rome, "at once the Paradise, / The grave, the city,
and the wilderness." Shelley has, in my opinion, harmonized
and reconciled the discordances and difficulties of the theme:
not by proposing a complete solution, indeed—the only possible
solution is to let the West Wind have its way—but by understanding, accepting, and realizing the dilemma in art.

In order fully to comprehend the complexity which Shelley
resolves, the weight of intellect and emotion which the poem
must carry, it is well to consider more thoroughly the central
symbol of the West Wind. In the context of the *Ode* it stands for
the spirit of revolution, or for revolutionary change; and we
have seen that, like Moses, it opens the way to the promised
land, without itself being permitted to enter. Its qualities, however, betray its relationship with more universal and more gra-
cious meanings. An unseen, irresistible power, it is a single door
which opens upon the central unity of all things, the very ful-
crum of Shelley's thought. It is an aspect of the master concept
of his most significant poetry.

The West Wind is an absolute and hidden power which
informs all things, while it is perceptible and to be imaged only
in its effects, like "the one Life within us and abroad" of Coleridge, or Wordsworth's

motion and a spirit, that impels
All thinking things, all objects of all thought,
And rolls through all things.

In the poetry of Shelley it is akin to the secret fire which inwardly illumines "the visioned maid" of *Alastor*. It is related to the "awful shadow" of intellectual beauty, which "floats through unseen among us"; and to the "imageless, deep truth" of *Prometheus Unbound*. In *Adonais* it becomes the eternal, the "burning fountain" whither shall return the creative genius of Keats:

... that sustaining Love
Which through the web of being blindly wove
By man and beast and earth and air and sea,
Burns bright or dim, as each are mirrors of
The fire for which all thirst.

In another guise, it is the skylark, the symbol of the poet, unseen, but inundating the sky with "profuse strains of unpremeditated art." Again, it has affinities with the unaccountable power of poetic inspiration as it is described in the *Defence of Poetry:* "the mind in creation is as a fading coal, which some invisible influence, like an inconstant wind, awakens to transitory brightness." The symbolism of the West Wind, in short, opens out into far-reaching associations, rich and deep in their freight of intellect and emotion.

Likewise rich in its imaginative ramifications is Shelley's development of the death and regeneration theme, into which is woven the myths of the seasons; of Christ, his resurrection, and of Judgment Day; and the imagery of the pastoral; all so skillfully harmonized that the shift from one to another is almost imperceptible. The leaves and the "winged seeds" will play their part in the great cyclical rebirth of spring, and the image of the seeds leads us also into the Christian resurrection of Easter. They "lie cold and low" until awakened by the gentle wind of spring, which suggests both the resurrection and Judgment Day as she blows "her clarion o'er the dreaming earth." The pastoral enters also, blended with the wind, "driving sweet buds like *flocks* to *feed* in air," linked to the Christian by the shepherd-sheep image, and merging once more with the rebirth of spring and nature, as the wind fills "with living hues and odors plain and hill." It may not perhaps be too fanciful to suggest yet another enriching association, harmonizing with the seasonal and religious myth alike; the West Wind is both Siva and Vishnu of the Hindu triad, destroyer and preserver together. Only Brahma, the creator, it is not.

Consequently, when in stanza 4 Shelley turns to the subjective and individual, his problem is given meaning and reference not merely by his attempted self-identification with the West Wind, but also by his relation of the individual to the ideological, cultural, religious, and natural wholes. By using the symbol of the West Wind, and by describing its effects upon leaf, cloud, and wave, he has realized and objectified the revolutionary ideal in nature; and by introducing the seasonal, religious, and pastoral myths he has softened and humanized a conception in itself perhaps a little rigoro... Then, in culmination, the personal binds the two aspects of the theme together. From the nature imagery of leaf-cloud-wave arises the prayer to be united with the wind: a union which will provide the means for the only sort of regeneration which Shelley—I should say modestly—deemed personally possible. That is, filled with an inspiration not of his own making or owning, his thoughts should be driven "like withered leaves to quicken a new birth"; his words should be scattered among mankind.

There has arisen of late years a strange disposition to deny a place to the subjective in poetry. This view I confess I do not fully understand; it would appear to lead to a hopeless confusion of the genres. An objective lyric seems to me as much a contradiction in terms as an actionless narrative, or a plotless drama. For those who are dismayed by the entrance of the poet upon the scene, however, it may be pointed out that in the *Ode to the West Wind* the personal element is an integral part of the design, as presumably could be established of any good lyric. The *Ode* is about self-abnegation, the absorption of the individual ego into a larger unity. It is, I think, then, more than a mere play on words to demand that there should be the imaginative realization of a self to be abnegated and absorbed. If the offering is to have significance, let it be prized by the giver.

The lines "I fall upon the thorns of life," and "A heavy

weight of hours has chained and bowed / One too like thee," which some have found objectionable, are obviously part of the imaginal design. The West Wind is free and uncontrollable. Shelley calls for a like though a lesser freedom—not egotistically, but through the power of self-dedication to a cause—to become the fitting instrument and medium of a voice, the trumpet of a prophecy not his own. That he introduces his own emotions, his sufferings, frailties, forebodings—serves to intensify the stress and increase the voltage of the poetic argument, to broaden its scope. Poems should end in reconciliation, but a unity too easily won is lacking in value. The personal stanzas of the *Ode to the West Wind* round out the expression of a problem that is felt and real. This reconciliation, to conclude, has as its materials the stress between the individual and the general, the actual and the ideal, each given its "ample room and verge enough." The resolvent is hope—hope tempered with humility—hope firmly-based in the revolutionary idealism symbolized by the West Wind, and in the immemorial logic of seasonal, religious, and pastoral myth.

7

Image and Imagelessness
A Limited Reading of *Prometheus Unbound*

A profitable reading of Shelley's *Prometheus Unbound* must rest, I think, upon a clear conception of its genre or kind. Whether one's judgment of it is favorable or unfavorable it should not be thought of as an anomaly: neither as a work of wild genius without antecedents in literary theory, or unfavorably as a formless and notionless fantasy. Its kind is romantic and Platonic, in senses which I shall try to explain; and the problems which it raises are central and fundamental. These problems will be treated here as problems of poetry, although they radiate outwards toward aesthetics and metaphysics.

Prometheus Unbound is a romantic drama of the imagination, as free as possible from the bounds of time, space, and matter, and governed only by the creative and artistic power and skill of the poet. This kind of drama has been defined by Coleridge in order to cope with Shakespeare, more particularly to enunciate appropriate principles for plays like *The Tempest*. The observation with which Coleridge begins is so appropriate to my thesis that I shall quote it at length:

> We call, for we see and feel, the swan and the dove both transcendently beautiful. As absurd as it would be to institute a comparison between their separate claims to beauty from any abstract rule common to both, without reference to the life and being of the animals themselves—say rather if, having first seen the dove, we abstracted its outlines, gave them a false generalization, called them principle or ideal of bird-beauty and then proceeded to criticize the swan or the eagle—not less absurd is it to pass judgment on the works of a poet on the mere ground that they have been called by the same class-name with the works of other poets of other times and circumstances, or any ground indeed save that of their inappropriateness to their own end and being, their want of significance, as symbol and physiognomy.[1]

I do not understand this passage as an appeal to the freedom of anarchy and absolute individualism; let it be noted that dove, eagle, and swan consitute classes, not individuals, in themselves. It is rather a salutary caution to make sure of the identity of the object you wish to account for. The romantic drama is a swan or an eagle—perhaps not a dove—which has its own principles and characteristics. Its peculiar function is to reconcile ideal truth and sensuous reality by the agency of the poetic imagination.

> The romantic poetry, the Shakespearian drama, appealed to the imagination rather than to the senses, and to the reason as contemplating our inward nature, the workings of the passions in their most retired recesses. But the reason, as reason, is independent of time and space; it has nothing to do with them. Hence the certainties of reason have been called *eternal truths*. . . . The reason is aloof from time and space; and imagination [has] an arbitrary control over both; and if only the poet have such power of exciting our internal emotions as to make us present to the scene in imagination chiefly, he acquires the right and privilege of using time and space as they exist in the imagination, obedient only to the laws which the imagination acts by.[2]

The reason here is of course the transcendental reason, which has immediate access to eternal, supersensuous truth. Since all art deals with time and space, it can enter into art only through the imagination. Thus Coleridge attempts to solve the problem and the paradox of art, that it is both sensuous and ideal. This problem, be it emphasized, is central and crucial; in his *History of Aesthetic*, for instance, Bernard Bosanquet treated it as the basic question of modern aesthetics.[3]

Prometheus Unbound is a gigantic effort to synthesize the abstract with the concrete, the ideal with the actual. It tries to express the inexpressible. Thus we should pay close attention to Shelley's discussion of character in his Preface. His Prometheus must be different from the Prometheus of Aeschylus, for Shelley is "averse from a catastrophe so feeble as that of reconciling the Champion with the Oppressor of mankind." He is unlike Milton's Satan, whom he also resembles, "because, in addition to courage, and majesty, and firm and patient opposition to omnipotent force, he is susceptible of being described as exempt from the taints of ambition, envy, revenge, and a desire for personal aggrandizement, which, in the Hero of *Paradise Lost*, interfere with the interest." *Interfere with the interest* is a very significant phrase. In other words Shelley will admit no imperfection whatever into his conception of the hero: a flaw would be not merely immoral but inartistic. In this he is fully accepting Plato's requirement that poetry should imitate unmixed virtue,[4] and rejecting Aristotle's hero who is great but faulty, as for example rash Oedipus or sulking Achilles.

All this, of course, is perfectly well known. What is novel in my argument I now affirm: the Platonic conception of literature is not a heresy, as most modern critics would have it, but one of two great streams, the Platonic and the Aristotelian, into which all "creative" writing may be divided. Its sanctions lie deep in fundamental and valuable human desires and aspirations. *Prometheus Unbound* is neither a fascinating sport nor a baseless fantasy; it is a supreme example of a permanent mode in literature. An important part of Shelley's value comes from his uncompromising and open-eyed acceptance of its terms. He expands and extends its possibilities, he is faced with new problems and faces them. The vital difficulty is to find an image for the idea of perfection, or how to attain to structure, movement, development. From the point of view of the reader, how is his interest to be attracted and maintained, how is his sympathy to be enlisted? Let us see how *Prometheus Unbound* deals with these problems.

It is natural to begin with Prometheus himself, as an imitation of unmixed virtue. Prometheus conquers Jupiter, his foe, not by force but by the power of forgiveness and love. The crucial action of the plot is his victory over himself, when he revokes his curse upon Jupiter. The question is, is there sufficient conflict and suspense in the plot to make it a genuine structure? Prometheus is good, and Jupiter is evil, and in Shelley's terms good must win by necessity. The answer to this question contains all other answers about *Prometheus Unbound*. The complete and inevitable victory of good is a tremendous imaginative effort and feat, which proceeds from a conscious and deliberate defiance of the actual. The central idea of the drama is the positive affirmation of the good. Its plot and structure come from confronting this idea with all the difficulties which oppose it, and drawing a conclusion which at once takes account of and contradicts our ordinary experience. Prometheus is both god and struggling man, who effectively dramatizes the affirmation and also the desperate mental strife to achieve it. And Jupiter, it is too infrequently noticed, is a worthy opponent, an imaginative conception of the first rank:

> The shape is awful, like the sound,
>   Clothed in dark purple, star-inwoven.
> A sceptre of pale gold
>   To stay steps proud, o'er the slow cloud
>   His veined hand doth hold.
> Cruel he looks, but calm and strong,
> Like one who does, not suffers wrong.
>
> (1. 233–239)

The fact that Jupiter is defeated only by necessity itself, in the person of Demogorgon, emphasizes his power and the drama of his fall. Jupiter serves also to embody the complexity of the hero Prometheus; he is associated with Prometheus in dignity, in isolation, expressed in repeated images of height and bareness in act 1, and in unalterable determination. One can think of him, in fact, as the masculine principle in Prometheus of courage and unlimited aspiration, but perverted and made evil from want of balance and control, which in Prometheus is supplied by Asia, the feminine principle of Love. The force of Jupiter is partly determined by the vigor of Shelley's conception of the good in Prometheus, which calls forth an equal power to oppose it. It has been noticed that there is an odd kind of Manichaeanism in Shelley, Ormuzd and Ahriman, light and darkness—and this is one way of explaining it.

Until the climax of *Prometheus Unbound* this opposition appears dramatically in the conception of a fatal bond between good and evil, in which every effort at advance becomes a retrogression, the aspiration of goodness is perverted into the fact of evil and misfortune. The Furies torture Prometheus by showing him visions of the future which unfailingly illustrate this prospect: Christ on the cross in the midst of the ghastly fruits of Christian bigotry, and the French Revolution, dedicated to truth, freedom, and love, but issuing forth in "the vintage-time for death and sin." This motif culminates in a remarkable figure of Love followed by Ruin as its shadow:

> As over wide dominions
> I sped, like some swift cloud that wings the wide air's wildernesses,
> That planet-crested shape swept by on lightning-braided pinions,
> Scattering the liquid joy of life from his ambrosial tresses:
> His footsteps paved the world with light; but as I passed 'twas fading,
> And hollow Ruin yawned behind: great sages bound in madness,
> And headless patriots, and pale youths who perished, unupbraiding
> Gleamed in the night.
>
> (1. 763–770)

In early scenes the principle of goodness (with the significant exception of Prometheus himself) is shown as a spirit "weak yet beautiful" (2. 3. 15), barely maintaining itself against the powers of evil, treasured partly for its very frailness and evanescence. Thus the spirits which comfort Prometheus after his torture by the furies are dim figures of human thought and not reality— "those subtle and fair spirits, / Whose homes are the dim caves of human thought" (ll. 658–659)—and their time is not yet.

This dimness and evanescence is, however, profoundly ambiguous, as in the nature of Platonic idealism it must be. When compared with concrete reality it is weak, but on the other hand a strength, the strength of the eternal, uncreated, and absolute Platonic forms. We have two measures of value: from the point of view of everyday, common sense reality and in quite another perspective from the point of view of idealism. The poetic implications of this ambiguity or ambivalence, which is central to *Prometheus Unbound*, can be more tellingly explored a little later in relation to imagery. At any rate, *Prometheus Unbound* is Platonic in its conception of character and of reality, but with a Platonism which comes to terms with literature. We may accept at face value Shelley's statement in his Preface:

Didactic poetry is my abhorrence. . . . My purpose has hitherto been simply to familiarise the highly refined imagination . . . with beautiful idealisms of moral excellence; aware that until the mind can love, and admire, and trust, and hope, and endure, reasoned principles of moral conduct are seeds cast upon the highway of life which the unconscious passenger tramples into dust, although they would bear the harvest of his happiness.

This is the central romantic reconciliation of beauty and truth, in which truth is made operative by the action of beauty upon the feelings. It suggests the effect of the water-snakes upon the mind of the Ancient Mariner. When the mariner is enabled to see the snakes as things of beauty, they become symbols of an organized, intelligible, and beneficent cosmos. The relationship is even closer. In *The Ancient Mariner* the perception of beauty leads to love:

A spring of love gushed from my heart
And I blessed them unawares.

So in *Prometheus Unbound* the spirit of love is inextricably bound up with beauty and vital truth.

It should be noticed that Shelley's "beautiful idealisms of moral excellence" are not allegorical but symbolic, in the modern sense of symbol adumbrated by Goethe, Coleridge, Yeats, and Croce. They are not arbitrary intellectual constructions, they are not exhaustible in terms of abstract ideas, but take on a life of their own from the imagination of the poet, difficult to define because entirely unprecedented and original. They are most comparable to the figures of Blake, which are susceptible of allegorical interpretation but nevertheless possess a final content and concreteness which defies analysis. They are not human by any common-sense definition of humanity, but they nevertheless are living, individual, and unique. Shelley is in some respects the antithesis of Blake: his is the generalizing imagination, Blake's the particularizing, but as prophetic and religious poets they meet in the middle. Shelley, commencing with the vision of the ideal, tries to bring his ideal into an intelligible relationship with recognizable reality. Blake, starting with the particular, moves toward a reconciliation with an all-embracing theory of cosmos. The hallmark of the prophetic poet, whose imagination is committed to constructing a cosmos above and differing from the world of average perception, is his use of repetitive patterns or motifs of imagery, symbols relatively unvarying in significance and not wholly dependent upon the poetic context in which they appear. In genuine poetry, however, they are not on the other hand wholly impervious to the demands of their context, but blend with it in at least a partial dramatic appropriateness. By this test the Shelley of *Prometheus Unbound* comes out better than the Blake of the *Prophetic Books*.

Shelley's figures, to discriminate, can be graded according to their relative concreteness and humanity. Prometheus is closest to human, Jupiter somewhat less so, while Demogorgon as necessity—what must be in the nature of things—is the most abstract. It should be pointed out, however, that in Demogorgon Shelley attempts with imaginative daring and complete awareness to solve his crucial problem in its extremest terms, to reconcile idea and image, after they have systematically been separated by the intellect, in an image of imagelessness:

> I see a mighty darkness
> Filling the seat of power, and rays of gloom
> Dart round, as light from the meridian sun,
> Ungazed upon and shapeless; neither limb,
> Nor form, nor outline; yet we feel it is
> A living Spirit.
>
> (2. 4. 2–7)

Demogorgon represents the ultimate in the testing of systematic thought by the demands of poetic imagination.

The imagery patterns of *Prometheus Unbound* disclose a good many facts about its theme, its structure, and its total meaning—that is, its entire intellectual, formal, and emotional impact upon the reader. I shall consider this imagery under three heads: images which develop the theme, images classified by representation (what they picture visually), and images of mental process. These heads are not logically exclusive, and are far from exhausting the content of the images which are classified by them. They can claim only to illuminate what seem to me to be the principal emphases of the imagery as a whole.

First, of images which develop the theme. Most noticeable at the beginning of *Prometheus Unbound* are images of deadness, immensity, and height:

> Nailed to this wall of eagle-baffling mountain,
> Black, wintry, dead, unmeasured; without herb,
> Insect, or beast, or shape and sound of life.
>
> (1. 20–22)

The images of immensity project the cosmic, almost infinite scope of the drama, unlimited in space and time, and yet only to be represented in physical and temporal terms. Thus the pangs of the tortured Prometheus are expressed in a kind of synecdoche:

Three thousand years of sleep-unsheltered hours,
And moments aye divided by keen pangs
Till they seemed years.

(1. 12–14)

The three thousand years are really a figure for a time which is just short of an eternity, and the two following lines introduce the concept of an imaginary time which takes precedence over the time of chronological measurement. Moments may seem years, they may even be longer than years, depending upon what they contain.

The images of deadness, most prevalent in act 1, stand for a dead world of the Fall, in which the evil principle predominates. Prometheus is nailed to his rock, he is separated from Asia, spirit of nature and love, and Jupiter the tyrant reigns. In this imagery Shelley is very close to Blake's vision of the fallen world of Urizen, dead, rocky, and broken into its separate elements—and Urizen, a spirit of cold and tyrannical reason, is very much like Jupiter. Closely associated with the dominant image of deadness are other images of hardness, of coldness, and of rending agony:

The crawling glaciers pierce me with the spears
Of their moon-freezing crystals, the bright chains
Eat with their burning cold into my bones.
Heaven's wingèd hound, polluting from thy lips
His beak in poison not his own, tears up
My heart; and shapeless sights come wandering by.
The ghastly people of the realm of dream,
Mocking me: and the Earthquake-fiends are charged
To wrench the rivets from my quivering wounds
When the rocks split and close again behind:

While from their loud abysses howling throng
The genii of the storm, urging the rage
Of whirlwind, and afflict me with keen hail.

(1. 31–43)

Images of tearing, splitting, and rending are remarkably frequent in act 1. They have several meanings. They symbolize the
illimitable agony of the tortured Prometheus, but also they
make two opposing suggestions from their recurring association
with earthquakes. One simply extends the pain of Prometheus
to the stony world of the Fall, with its towering peaks and
subterranean fires. Another implication, however, foreshadows
the coming destruction of the apparently solid and invulnerable
realm of Jupiter. This suggests on the one hand the vast imprisoned Titans, chained but still rebellious beneath Tartarus; on
the other it calls to mind Blake's Orc, the fettered spirit of
Revolution. Here it may be politic to remark that Shelley's
conclusion avoids and transcends the implication of his image
through Prometheus' act of love and self-mastery. The pain and
incipient violence of the world of the Fall is imaged also in
extreme cold and heat, which are fused as one in the "burning
cold" of line 33. Of the two cold predominates, in keeping with
the pattern of winter and oppression, but their association corresponds with the association of mountain and earthquake in
suggesting that extreme incurs extreme, and that their conjunction is evil.

Opposed to the images of the fallen world are images of
regeneration, primarily images of dawn, spring, and growth.
These run throughout the play—one is present in the opening
stage direction—but naturally are fuller and more decisive in
its later stages. In the opening scene "morning slowly breaks."
At the beginning of act 2 Asia's reunion with Prometheus is
foreshadowed by lovely and unsettling exhalations of spring:

(From all the blasts of heaven thou hast descended:
Yes, like a spirit, like a thought, which makes
Unwonted tears throng to the horny eyes,

And beatings haunt the desolated heart,
Which should have learnt repose.)

(2. 1. 1–5)

and by the simultaneous appearance of dawn and the messenger
Panthea:

. . . hear I not
The Aeolian music of her sea-green plumes
Winnowing the crimson dawn?

(2. 1. 25–27)

Images of growth it is appropriate to discuss along with the main
image of organic life, which is involved with the general movement toward a world redeemed and physically transformed.

This image is related to the character of the Earth herself,
first seen as an elemental mother, and finally transfigured in the
last act. In act 1 the process is anticipated:

I am the Earth,
Thy mother; she within whose stony veins,
To the last fibre of the loftiest tree
Whose thin leaves trembled in the frozen air,
Joy ran, as blood within a living frame,
When thou [Prometheus] didst from her bosom,
     like a cloud
Of glory, arise, a spirit of keen joy!

(1. 152–158)

An inorganic and petrified structure is warmed, inspirited, and
transformed into a sentient organic body. Again

I hear, I feel;
Thy lips are on me, and their touch runs down
Even to the adamantine central gloom
Along these marble nerves; 'tis life, 'tis joy,
And, through my withered, old, and icy frame

The warmth of an immortal youth shoots down
Circling.

(3. 3. 84–90)

In act 4 the Earth and the Spirit of Earth are joined in a climactic synthesizing image in which the inorganic and organic are fused. Motion and stillness, spirit and matter, unity and complexity, sensation and idea are all compressed in a single amazing whole, whose basic elements are the earth imagined as an orb and as a mythologized human figure:

Within the orb itself,

Pillowed upon its alabaster arms,
Like to a child o'erwearied with sweet toil,
On its own folded wings, and wavy hair,
The Spirit of the Earth is laid asleep.

(4. 261–265)[5]

Among what I have called images of representation, I shall notice as characteristic the cavern, the eagle or vulture and the serpent, the river, the boat, and the veil. There are two caverns in *Prometheus Unbound*, the cavern of Demogorgon and the cave to which Prometheus retires with Asia, Panthea, and Ione, when his great task is happily completed. The cavern of Demogorgon stands for the utmost depths of the human mind, which must be plumbed before man can be redeemed. The conception would please a psychiatrist, but this cavern should not be flatly identified with the unconscious. In relative terms it certainly stands for instinct and feeling. It is significant that Asia, a comparatively passive symbol of nature and love, should be summoned to this cavern, and not Prometheus, who is a masculine symbol of reason and inhabits the heights. The cavern is the complement in depth of the sky-towering intellect. Shelley, in the union of Prometheus and Asia, makes clear that the two must be fused. The second cave, the abode of ideal happiness, has been criticized as evoking too calm and static a picture of experience, inconsistent with cosmic and high endeavor. This question, of course, invokes the whole problem of imagining the millennium. There is space here only to suggest cursorily that in the total context of the play this cavern impresses one as being only a resting place upon a journey, or one element of an archetypal pattern of withdrawal and return. Detailed examination of act 4 would show in actuality a substantial group of images of struggle and progress.

The Manichaean and Gnostic symbol of the vulture and serpent appears only once in all its elements in *Prometheus Unbound*, but the one instance, the downfall of Jupiter, has decided force:

> Sink with me then,
> We two will sink on the wide waves of ruin,
> Even as a vulture and a snake outspent
> Drop, twisted in extricable fight,
> Into a shoreless sea.
>
> (3. 1. 70–74)

This image is striking primarily, of course, because of its reversal of terms. The serpent, not the bird of heaven, is the hero and victor. The simplest explanation for this reversal is Shelley's democratic feelings, which make the lower the good, and upset our usual notions of hierarchy. Heaven, as with Blake, is the symbol of tyranny and repression. Since this particular snake is a metaphor for Demogorgon, we may say that here the nature of things itself is demanding and getting back its own. The image, one may remark, is genuinely tragic, for the struggling bird is a regal creature of dignity and power.

The related symbols of the river and the boat, so frequently to be found in Shelley, represent aspiration, desire, synthesis, and conclusion. The river may flow into a cavern, or else into the sea. In *Prometheus Unbound* it is used most notably as, first, the medium of an irresistible attraction and, second, of a progression to the ultimate of Demogorgon's cave:

To the deep, to the deep,
  Down, down!
Through the shade of sleep,
Through the cloudy strife
Of Death and of Life;
Through the veil and the bar
Of things which seem and are,
Even to the steps of the remotest throne,
  Down, down!

(2. 3. 54–62)

The boat appears in Asia's famous lyric,

My soul is an enchanted boat,
Which, like a sleeping swan, doth float
Upon the silver waves of thy sweet singing.

Its destiny is once again ultimate reality: it passes (in this instance backwards and downwards and through) Age, Manhood, Youth, and "shadow-peopled Infancy," through Death and Birth themselves, to arrive at last in "A paradise" (2. 5. 72–110). This boat journey in Shelley is habitually accompanied by synaesthetic fusions of thought with sensation, and transferences among sensations themselves. Water, motion, and music are generally equated, and referred to the motion and the vibration of the spirit.

The veil image, perhaps the dominant image of Shelley's poetry, is on the borderline of my distinction between representation and mental process. As veil itself it is representational, but the element of mind, because of the tenuousness of its imaginal content, is about equally prominent with its visual qualities. Its ramifications symbolize the problems and complexities of the central theme. Most simply the veil is a concealment of the truth, which must be torn aside. Thus the fallen world of Jupiter is a veil, which when discarded reveals the true and transfigured world of Prometheus:

The painted veil, by those who were, called life,
Which mimicked, as with colours idly spread,
All men believed or hoped, is torn aside;
The loathsome mask has fallen.

(3. 4. 190–193)

But equally with this confident image appears another, more complex development, which contains both the search for truth and the difficulty of locating it. It asks the question, does truth exist without a veil, or, given reality as a whole, which element of it is the original, the deep truth? It may at this point be the truest economy to cite for comment a single lengthy passage. This is the dream of Panthea, in which Prometheus appears to her transfigured:

>   . . . his pale wound-worn limbs
> Fell from Prometheus, and the azure night
> Grew radiant with the glory of that form
> Which lives unchanged within, and his voice fell
> Like music which makes giddy the dim brain,
> Faint with intoxication of keen joy:
> "Sister of her whose footsteps pave the world
> With loveliness—more fair than aught but her,
> Whose shadow thou art—lift thine eyes on me!"
> I lifted them: the overpowering light
> Of that immortal form was shadowed o'er
> By love; which from his soft and flowing limbs,
> And passion-parted lips, and keen, faint eyes
> Steamed forth like vaporous fire; an atmosphere
> Which wrapped me in its all-dissolving power,
> As the warm aether of the morning sun
> Wraps ere it drinks some cloud of wandering dew.
> I saw not, heard not, moved not, only felt
> His presence flow and mingle through my blood
> Till it became his life, and his grew mine,
> And I was thus absorbed, until it passed,
> And like the vapours when the sun sinks down,
> Gathering again in drops upon the pines,

And tremulous as they, in the deep night
My being was condensed; and as the rays
Of thought were slowly gathered, I could hear
His voice, whose accents lingered ere they died
Like footsteps of weak melody.

(2. 1. 62–89)

In the opening lines (62–65) the veil is the appearance which conceals the truth, the eternal Prometheus within, a glory and an overpowering light. A new veil, however, is immediately substituted; the light is "shadowed o'er by love," which tempers its insupportable pure brilliance. This love, it will be noticed, is itself a fire (l. 75), and possesses an "all-dissolving power" of its own (l. 76). It is suggested that *this* power is endurable, unlike the naked glory of the earlier vision of Prometheus. Love, in fact, is a veil of vaporous fire which tempers and intermediates between the truth and its beholder. Panthea is momentarily overcome and absorbed, but beneficently, gently,

As the warm aether of the morning sun
Wraps ere it drinks some cloud of wandering dew.

The veil, then, hiding the truth in one aspect, becomes an addition to it, a new and fuller vision of it, from the effects of a fusion of truth and the veil. The complexity of the figure calls forth a further consideration. Its visual qualities lead one on to seek for a final truth, isolated, elemental, and unmistakable— what might be called an ultimate certainty for which the other parts of the figure are only a cloak and a concealment. But the deep truth, penetrate as one will, is still pervasive and difficult, impossible to isolate. As light and fire it is omnipresent, and it cannot be distinguished from form (l. 64) and shape (l. 71). The image of the transfigured Prometheus is living and in its life indivisible.

As an image of ultimate reality it is overpowering. Panthea is enwrapped, dissolved, absorbed; her identity is lost within it. This self-abandonment, however, is only temporary. The moment passes, her being is condensed, the rays of her thought are once again gathered and recorded (ll. 86–87). The vision past, equilibrium reestablished, what is left to her of it? Not the vision itself, but an aftertaste, a memory—as much of truth as can be grasped and held. This is Shelley's "narrowing image,"[6] in which the truth, receding, dwindles to a point,

> Keen as are the arrows
>   Of that silver sphere,
>   Whose intense lamp narrows
>   In the white dawn clear
> Until we hardly see—we feel that it is there.
>
> (*To a Skylark*, ll. 21–25)

The narrowing image has two important implications. It is a dramatic expression of the search for truth pursued to its furthest point, beyond which it is impossible to go. In its other development it is "residual"; it is the mind's attempt to hold what it has momentarily gained, and the mind's victorious defeat. What is left is only an echo, lingering "Like footsteps of far melody," but it nevertheless constitutes an advance, an enlargment of the spirit. The passage quoted above presents an evolution of Panthea's being: overmastered, she returns to herself, increased in insight and wisdom.

Here I conceive myself to be dealing with a subject of great importance in evaluating Shelley's poetry. (I do not conceive myself to be dealing with it definitively.) Anti-Shelley criticism has had much to say of Shelley's "helpless surrender to his own emotions," his unwholesome ecstasies, his dissolutions and incoherences. These incoherences have never been perceptible to me, but I have at least some notion of what is meant by the charge. Panthea's quoted speech is an instance of what gives rise to it in the poetry of Shelley. No final and decisive answer to it is possible, since the answer must rest upon both the surrounding context of *Prometheus Unbound* and the context of all Shelley's verse. To these, indeed, one would need to add one's total impression of Shelley from all the evidences of his biography. The answer, then, cannot be certain, but it is nevertheless unquestionably the duty of the critic to give it. Shelley is expressing not a surrender, not a passive emotion, but the result of intellectual effort pushed to its furthest reaches, with all the difficulties and dangers which are involved in it. He presents a full cycle of the confrontation, of the struggle, and of the victorious defeat of the human spirit at full stretch. What seems superficially to be formlessness and the shattering of order is really the synthesis of form and formlessness, of expansion and determination, of image and imagelessness. As such, it is the wholly consistent result of absorbing into art a system of thought which has not been, to put it mildly, without influence in the world, and is not lightly to be banished by even the most confident criticism.

8

Dante and Shelley's *Adonais*

This study has its origin in an unpublished commentary on
Adonais written in the margins of a copy of the first edition in
1822 by Shelley's friend John Taaffe. Taaffe, the author of
a notable commentary on the *Divine Comedy*, was peculiarly
sensitive to Dante at the time, and he found parallels in
Adonais, especially to the *Paradiso*, that have gone largely undis-
covered in print to this day, despite the valuable work of
Carlos Baker in his *Shelley's Major Poetry* and more recently of
Glenn O'Malley in *Shelley and Synesthesia*. Taaffe's achievement
is substantial, and my own interest in the Dante-Shelley
relationship was brought about by his commentary. My present effort, however, is directed primarily toward the interpretation of *Adonais* itself, and my exhibitions of evidence are
confined to the *Paradiso*, more congenial to Shelley than either
the *Inferno* or the *Purgatorio*. This essay mentions only a fraction
of the instances in which resemblances are present, and I
take the liberty of omitting, as too well known to require

distinction, the external evidence of Shelley's familiarity with the *Divine Comedy* in the original and in Cary's translation.

It is curious that Shelley most resembles Dante in passages that are thoroughly characteristic of his own abiding qualities and preoccupations; he appears to use him for corroboration rather than at absolute need. Thus, perhaps since both are visionaries, he echoes Dante in one of his most Shelleyan and romantic statements in *A Defence of Poetry*, on the inadequacy of the word to the original conception. Dante, arriving in his last canto at the ultimate revelation of the Trinity, exclaims,

O quanto é corto il dire, e come fuoco
Al mio concetto!

(Paradiso 33. 121–122)

"Alas," he says, "how short and feeble is the word for my conception." So Shelley habitually feels the presence of a gap between the original inspiration and the possibility of verbal expression. "The mind in creation is as a fading coal, which some invisible influence, like an inconstant wind, awakens to transitory brightness. . . . Could this influence be durable in its original purity and force, it is impossible to predict the greatness of the results; but when composition begins, inspiration is already on the decline, and the most glorious poetry that has ever been communicated to the world is probably a feeble shadow of the original conceptions of the poet." The special bearing of these passages upon the present issue, however, is that both the *Paradiso* and *Adonais* seek the ultimate vision, and both poets concede that this vision is ineffable and can only be partially expressed in images and symbols. For Dante the Trinity is three whirling gyres of different colors within the one white light; for Shelley,

. . . burning through the inmost veil of Heaven,
The soul of Adonais, like a star,
Beacons from the abode where the Eternal are.

(55. 493–495)

Shelley's image suggests the most comprehensive resemblance of all. His basic image is a figure drowned or obscured in its own light, which struggles with the shape that realizes it, as does the effect of sublimity in Longinus, in the figure whose brilliance strives with the modifying shape of its appropriateness. Such images are also the central visual device of the *Paradiso*, in which light itself is the master image. Thus the first experience of the Empyrean Heaven is clothed in a garb which considering my point of view I hope I may be pardoned for calling highly Shelleyan:

As a quick flash of lightning shattering
The visual spirits so that it bereaves
The eye of strength to sense yet stronger sights,
So round me shone a living cloak of light
And left me wrapped in such a glowing veil
That nothing else took shape before my eyes.
                    (*Paradiso* 30. 46–51, trans. Thomas Bergin)

One assumes, too, that Shelley's frequent "splendors" derive from Dante's *splendori*, consistently used in the *Paradiso* for personification:

Behold, another of those splendors came
Toward me, and waxing outwardly more bright
Revealed his eagerness to bring me joy.
                                        (9. 13–15)

So, in *Adonais*,

Another Splendour on his mouth alit,
That mouth, whence it was wont to draw the breath
Which gave it strength to pierce the guarded wit,
And pass into the panting heart beneath
With lightning and with music: the damp death
Quenched its caress upon his icy lips.
                                        (12. 100–105)

These lines also present another parallel, in the association of music and light. The *Paradiso* contains several instances specifically of lightning linked to music, and more pervasively harmony and light in the music of the luminous spheres of the heavens and the angelic choir.

Adonais and the *Paradiso* are vision-poems, and in their pursuit of final revelation they are of course also poems of the quest, journeys of the ship upon a great and perhaps boundless ocean. Dante warns his readers that few of them are fitted for this voyage:

O ye who in your little bark have come,
After my ship that cuts the wave with song,
Eager to hear, O turn ye back again
To look on your own shores, nay set not forth
On the wide Ocean sea, lest it may hap
That, losing sight of me, ye go astray.
The sea I range was never coursed before:
Minerva blows; Apollo guides me on
And the nine Muses point me out the Bears.

(2. 1–9)

The comparable lines in *Adonais* have both significant likenesses and differences:

The breath whose might I have invoked in song
Descends on me; my spirit's bark is driven,
Far from the shore, far from the trembling throng
Whose sails were never to the tempest given;
The massy earth and sphered skies are riven!
I am borne darkly, fearfully, afar;
Whilst burning through the inmost veil of Heaven,
The soul of Adonais, like a star,
Beacons from the abode where the Eternal are.

(55. 487–495)

Dante expresses the mingled confidence and humility of the

epic poet at the beginning of his endeavors. One thinks of Milton's

> advent'rous song
> That with no middle flight intends to soar
> Above the Aonian Mount, while it pursues
> Things unattempted yet in Prose or Rhyme.

And doubtless also of his "fit audience though few." Words-worth, somewhat closer to Shelley in his epic fragment of *The Recluse*, has the same confidence (Blake thought it unbearable presumption), and the same sense of the enormous difficulties of his task:

> Urania, I shall need
> Thy guidance, or a greater Muse, if such
> Descend to earth or dwell in highest heaven!
> For I must tread on shadowy ground, must sink
> Deep—and, aloft ascending, breathe in worlds
> To which the heaven of heavens is but a veil.
> All strength—all terror, single or in bands,
> That ever was put forth in personal form—
> Jehovah—with his thunder, and the choir
> Of shouting angels, and the empyreal thrones—
> I pass them unalarmed.

Shelley's journey, however, is lyric and also dramatic, rather than epic. His bark is like Dante's, but it reminds us of other boats in his own poetry; the boat of the Poet in *Alastor*, which conveys him over seas, rivers, and through winding caverns finally to death, or "My soul is an enchanted boat," in Asia's song in *Prometheus Unbound*. Once again a possible indebtedness to Dante finds Shelley most deeply himself, and taking what is essentially his own by right of imaginative conquest.

In Shelley's case it is impossible to ignore the dramatic coincidence of his own death at sea, so soon to follow *Adonais*.

Thus, perhaps overinfluenced, one finds a deeper and more personal dread and revulsion, along with exaltation, in his "I am borne darkly, fearfully afar." Dante, though ranging unknown seas, is guided by Minerva, Apollo, and all nine Muses, and his destination is sure. Shelley's haven is perhaps more distant, and cetainly a more precarious prospect. Further, it is out of time and space—"The massy earth and sphered skies are riven"—in a sense more radical than Dante's Empyrean, which though beyond the physical universe is approached by regular steps ascending through the spheres. The effect in Shelley (and one recalls that Wordsworth *passes* the empyreal thrones) is violent, paradoxical, and romantic.

To return to our basic points of relationship, light and the quest for the ultimate, we can oversimplify by saying that Dante's progress in the *Paradiso* is hierarchical, while Shelley's in *Adonais* is dialectical. Dante's is the expanding vision, a perception altered by degrees to conform to the gradually increasing light as he ascends through sphere after sphere toward the ultimate Empyrean. His is a cosmos of order and degree, in which everything is consummately in its proper place, according to the system of the Angelic Doctor. Shelley's vision also expands, but it is a protean shape-changer; it advances through transformations and oppositions. Dante is wholly concerned with light in the *Paradiso*, while Shelley touches constantly on darkness. Stated flatly, Dante's is the characteristic order of the Middle Ages and the Renaissance; Shelley's evolves from the romantic reconciliation of opposites. In *Adonais* he advances, as Earl Wasserman has said, by "progressive revelation." During the poem there is a continuous process of alteration as one insight after another gives way before a fuller vision. The sunlight of physical life must yield to the darkness of death, which yet is the one white light of the eternal, and the night of death in which suns perish cannot vanquish the immortal stars.

Modern interpreters of *Adonais* have found crucial significance in its synesthetic fusion of the flower and the star, especially as the regeneration of springtime, with its "quickening life from the Earth's heart" (19. 164), must eventually give way to a time that will "leave to its kindred lamps the spirit's awful night" (29. 261). Shelley subtly foreshadows the transition in stanza 20, in the very act of celebrating the renewed life of nature in the cycle of the seasons.

The leprous corpse, touched by this spirit tender,
Exhales itself in flowers of gentle breath;
Like incarnations of the stars, when splendour
Is changed to fragrance, they illumine death.

(20. 172–175)

In Dante's approach to the Empyrean,

A flowing radiance like a river shaped
I saw all golden glowing between banks
Adorned with all the wondrous blooms of spring.
From out this river living sparks came forth
And fell into the flowers on every side,
Seeming like precious rubies set in gold.
Then, as if drunk with all the fragrances,
They plunged again into the wondrous pool
And at each plunge another drop sprang forth.

(30. 60–68)

Shelley's "when splendour / Is changed to fragrance" doubt-less involves a more radical unification than Dante's "as if drunk with all the fragrances." John Crowe Ransom and others have accused Shelley of overaddiction to the cautious "like" and "as if" of simile. If so, here he goes all the way with his transformation from "splendour" to "fragrance," to incur instead Irving Babbitt's reproaches for committing the sin of synesthesia. Actually in his poetry the idea and the image are harder to separate than they generally are in Dante, since Dante is a conscious and consistent allegorist whose method is to clothe essences with visible materials.

It is interesting to find that Shelley's Platonic or Neoplatonic conception of a continuous spiritual evolution in being, expressed in the climactic stanzas of *Adonais*, is anticipated on several occasions in the *Paradiso*. Under the beneficent compulsion of the One, created things are forced to attain to their full potentialities:

> the one Spirit's plastic stress
> Sweeps through the dull dense world, compelling there,
> All new successions to the forms they wear;
> Torturing the unwilling dross that checks its flight
> To its own likeness, as each mass may bear.
>
> (43. 381–385)

As Ellsworth Barnard points out, Shelley attributes a like belief to "The Greek philosophers" in his essay "On the Devil and Devils," and there is an exposition of it in Plato's *Statesman*. A later stanza invokes

> That light whose smile kindles the Universe,
> That Beauty in which all things work and move,
> That Benediction which the eclipsing Curse
> Of birth can quench not, that sustaining Love
> Which through the web of being blindly wove
> By man and beast and earth and air and sea,
> Burns bright or dim, as each are mirrors of
> The fire for which all thirst.
>
> (54. 478–485)

The *Paradiso*, on its part, commences with the statement that

> The glory of the Mover of all things,
> Perfusing the whole Universe, yet glows
> More brightly in some parts, in others less.
>
> (1. 1–3)

Somewhat later Beatrice explains to the poet that

> All things that are have order
> Among themselves; 'tis this that is the form
> Which makes the universe like unto God.
> And here the loftier creatures see the stamp
> Of the eternal Worth which is the goal
> For which the norm aforesaid was designed.
> Under this order things of every kind
> Do all incline, each following its lot,
> Nearer or less near to their Principle.
>
> (1. 103–111)

In canto 2 Dante asks on the moon the reason for the spots on its surface as seen from the earth. Beatrice explains this by the analogy of the stars, which, deriving their brilliance ultimately from God, reflect this brilliance in proportion to the capacities of their own natures. In canto 13 St. Thomas informs Dante that all things are emanations of the divine idea, which, though remaining one, is refracted in many manifestations. This reminds us still of the notion of potentiality under discussion, but likewise carries forward to a different version of the One and the many:

> The One remains, the many change and pass;
> Heaven's light forever shines, Earth's shadows fly;
> Life, like a dome of many-coloured glass,
> Stains the white radiance of Eternity,
> Until Death tramples it to fragments.
>
> (*Adonais*, 52. 460–464)

As has been suggested, Shelley's method is dialectical, with the unity of the One evolving from diversity. Dante's scheme, with its ascending heavens, is in comparison prearranged, a matter not of becoming but of being. This, by contrast, helps to illuminate the romantic process in which the poem itself, *Adonais*, or *Kubla Khan*, or the *Ode on Intimations of Immortality*, is the instrument and organizer of the poet's thought.

To recapitulate: in the *Paradiso* Dante, conducted by Beatrice, moves steadily upward toward the Empyrean Heaven, which is beyond time and space, through spheres of ever-increasing light: the Moon, Mercury, Venus, the Sun, Mars, Jupiter, Saturn, the Fixed Stars, and the Primum Mobile, the outer rim of the physical universe. As he ascends his vision gradually alters and expands, in accord with the greater and greater wonders he beholds. The ascent, indeed, *must* be gradual, or as mere mortal man he would be blasted with excess of light. Thus, in canto 23,

> The lucent substance shone so clearly through
> The living light upon my face that I
> Had sight not strong enough to take it in.
> O Beatrice, my sweet and cherished guide! . . .
> She said to me: "What overwhelms you here
> Is virtue against which no shield avails. . . ."
> Like to the fire in a cloud, expanding
> So that no longer checked it rushes forth . . .
> My mind, grown greater by its nourishment
> On such rich fare, burst its own bonds apart
> And cannot now recall what it became.
> "Open your eyes and look on what I am;
> Such things you've seen that you are now become
> Of strength sufficient to sustain my smile."
>
> (ll. 30–48)

Again, in canto 30, Dante looks upward through the Primum Mobile to the floor of heaven. What he sees gradually changes, as more and more is revealed to him. Beatrice tells him that what he sees at first

> Are shadowed prefaces of their true sense.
> Not that these things are bitter in themselves,
> But rather through defect in you, in that
> Your vision may not yet so proudly soar.
>
> (ll. 79–81)

96

Dante now drinks of the heavenly river of grace, and all is altered for him, as if the mask has been withdrawn from reality.

No sooner had my eyelids' outer eaves
Drunk of it, than straightway it seemed to me
Its length was changed to roundness. Furthermore,
As people wearing masks seem otherwise
Than what they were, once they have taken off
The semblances wherein their own were hid,
So into yet more jocund festive throngs
The flowers and flames were changed and I could see
Clear set before me both the courts of heaven.

(ll. 88–96)

Reflecting upon this general pattern, one notes the process by which veil after veil is stripped away from the innermost reality, and that at times the light itself is a veil, remembering that the veil image is dominant over all others in Shelley's poetry, including *Adonais*. Less important, perhaps, but still interesting, is the elementary fact of the astronomical spheres of Dante's heavens, in relation to Shelley's complex of sun, darkness, and star in *Adonais*. In Shelley's poem, however, alteration and expansion of vision are more radical; they evolve through apparent contradictions, as it were through an ascending series of hypotheses, in each of which an element is kept while the rest is discarded.

Adonais deals with the central problem of elegy, the physical death of a being worthy of immortality. Shelley commences, like Milton in *Lycidas*, with the comfort of ritual and ceremony. Adonais lies on his flower-bedecked bier; about him, as in Bion and Moschus, "the Loves lie lamenting." The implications of the living flowers and the dews that enliven them carry us on to the physical rebirth of springtime, bursting from earth's heart:

As it has ever done, with change and motion,
From the great morning of the world when first

God dawned on Chaos; in its steam immersed,
The lamps of Heaven flash with a softer light.

(19. 165–168)

The physical cycle of rebirth must be rejected, but "the lamps of Heaven" and, as we have seen, the flower-star fusion (*"incarnations* of the stars") pave the way for another vision. We move from sphere to sphere as the physical sun, the symbol of the poet Adonais, sets in death, but becomes in the spirit an immortal star.

"The sun comes forth, and many reptiles spawn;
He sets, and each ephemeral insect then
Is gathered into death without a dawn,
And the immortal stars awake again;
So is it in the world of living men:
A godlike mind soars forth, in its delight
Making earth bare and veiling heaven, and when
It sinks, the swarms that dimmed or shared its light
Leave to its kindred lamps the spirit's awful night."

(29. 253–261)

In the shift of vision darkness is first a veil, the illusion of death, and then the stripping away of illusion, the background for the true light of the star, reality itself. In another perspective darkness is pure light as with St. John of the Cross and his "dark night of the soul," and not to be distinguished from "that light whose smile kindles the Universe." But in the star pattern it appears as the night of eternity, an image necessary to preserve the individuality of the final incarnation.

And thus we return to the ultimate vision of Keats-Adonais, burning like a star through the inmost veil of heaven: "Dust to the dust, but the pure Spirit shall flow / Back to the burning fountain whence it came." In keeping with the purposes of elegy, he is at last fully embodied, his potentialities realized, pure light without shadow, pure spirit without alloy of material grossness. I conclude with a final significant parallel in the

Paradiso, itself a reference to Plato's *Timaeus:*

Further occasion of perplexity
Springs from the seeming of these souls to turn
Back to the stars, as Plato's word affirms.

(4. 22–24)

"Secondo la sentenza di Platone." John Taaffe, in his comments
of 1822, remarks that "according to Plato the various spiritual
essences are regents over various spheres. He calls those regents
ideas, and Christians, changing the name, but not the thing, call
them Angels." Let us remember, then, the figure of the "kingless
sphere" that awaits Adonais, "silent alone amid an Heaven of
Song."

9

Keats's *Ode to a Nightingale*

The *Nightingale* ode has been judiciously dealt with from inside the tradition of Keats scholarship by such experts as Sir Sidney Colvin, Ernest de Sélincourt, Douglas Bush, and H. W. Garrod. Reinterpretations by Brooks and Warren, by Thomas and Brown, by Allen Tate, F. R. Leavis, Marshall McLuhan, G. Wilson Knight, Albert Guérard, Jr., and others, have brought the *Ode* into contact with current critical theories. In following them here I can, I believe, be most useful by steering something of a middle course between the modern and traditional: with, however, an unusual emphasis upon general English romanticism. My explication, then, will consider the *Ode to a Nightingale* as a romantic poem, and will venture some exposition of its romantic principles. I shall also try to bear in mind the implications of recent criticism.

The *Nightingale* is a romantic poem of the family of *Kubla Khan* and *The Eve of St. Agnes* in that it describes a choice and rare experience, intentionally remote from the commonplace. Nowadays we sometimes underrate the skill required for this

100

sort of thing. The masters of romantic magic were aware that ecstasy, for example, is not adequately projected by crying, "I am ecstatic!" Keats gets his effects in the *Nightingale* by framing the consummate moment in oppositions, by consciously emphasizing its brevity; he sets off his ideal by the contrast of the actual. The principal stress of the poem is a struggle between ideal and actual: inclusive terms which, however, contain more particular antitheses of pleasure and pain, of imagination and commonsense reason, of fulness and privation, of permanence and change, of nature and the human, of art and life, freedom and bondage, waking and dream. These terms are of course only expedients; they are products of "that false secondary power which multiplies distinctions," and I fear might easily be multiplied still further. I defend them as the best I am able to frame, and as necessary for analysis.

The drugged, dull pain in lines 1–4 is a frame and a contrast for the poignant pleasure of the climax; at the same time, it is inseparable from it. "Extremes meet," as Coleridge was fond of saying, and as Keats also has said elsewhere in *A Song of Opposites* and the *Ode on Melancholy*. They meet because they *are* extremes, as very hot and cold water are alike to the touch—their extremity is their affinity—and because of a romantic prepossession to unity of experience, which in Keats was a matter of temperament as well as of conviction. Both pleasure and pain are deliberately heightened, and meet in a common intensity. The pain is the natural sequel of "too much happiness." the systole to the diastole of joy.

'Tis not through envy of thy happy lot,
But being too happy in thine happiness.

Despite this disavowal of envy, perhaps the envy is about the same as being "too happy." The felicity which is permanent in the nightingale is transient and therefore excessive in the poet. It is too heavy a burden to be borne more than briefly, and dangerous in its transience. Its attractions make everyday living ugly by contrast. Cleanth Brooks has defined as the theme of the poem "the following paradox: the world of the imagination offers a release from the painful world of actuality, yet at the same time it renders the world of actuality more painful by contrast."[1] Allen Tate has called the *Nightingale* "an emblem of one limit of our experience: the impossibility of synthesizing, in the order of experience, the antinomy of the ideal and the real."[2] Both statements strike into the crucial dilemma of the romantic imagination, a basic donnée of the romantic poet which he may turn to his advantage or his bane as he is able to cope with it. Good romantic poems, like *Kubla Khan* and the *Nightingale*, define this dilemma, dramatize it, and transform it to a source of strength. Such poetry accepts the risk to get at the value, in full awareness of the issues. To affirm either that the difficulty itself is avoidable, or that it could be definitively solved by a properly framed discourse, would be to talk of something other than poetry.

The theme of stanza 2 is plenitude. The ideal lies in fulness. The nightingale sings "in full-throated ease," the longed-for beaker is "full of the warm South, / Full of the true, the blushful Hippocrene." This fulness contrasts with the sad satiety of stanza 3, "where but to think is to be full of sorrow"; it is modulated in the "embalmed darkness" of stanza 5, in richness of sensuous texture; and it ends in stanza 6 in a climactic fulness of song:

While thou art pouring forth thy soul abroad
    In such an ecstasy!

The fabric of stanza 2 is too fine for common wear, a happiness too great, a conjunction of circumstances impossibly appropriate. The draught of vintage has been "cooled *a long age* in the *deep-delved* earth," the quite un-Miltonic fount of the Muses is "the *true*, the *blushful* Hippocrene," and the beaker is brimfull, with "purple-stained mouth." Such concentration of effect is probably what Keats had in mind when he advised Shelley to "load every rift with ore." Here it is used to image a Golden Age, before Jove reigned, of fulness, gusto, ease, and freedom. To achieve this ideal, however, the imagination builds upon the finite actual. The passage is deliberately pure and quintessential—the ore has been refined—and in its purity delicately defiant and mirthful. Such writing is a romantic equivalent of metaphysical wit. It differs from the metaphysical mode in its more thorough subordination to the total meaning.

The draught of vintage, itself an instrument of imagination, symbolizes an imaginative escape from actuality. The longing to "fade away into the forest dim" is in order to avoid another kind of fading away, the melancholy dissolutions of change and physical decay. The world of stanza 3 is the antitype of the golden world of stanza 2: for ease is substituted "the weariness, the fever, and the fret," for plenitude "a few sad, last grey hairs." It is a world of privation, "where youth grows pale, and spectre-thin, and dies."

In his judicious reading of the *Ode to a Nightingale* Allen Tate finds little to say for this stanza. It is bad eighteenth-century personification, without on the one hand Pope's precision, or the energy of Blake on the other. "It gives us," says Mr. Tate, "a 'picture' of common reality, in which the life of man is all mutability and frustration. But here if anywhere in the poem the necessity to dramatize time or the pressure of actuality, is paramount. *Keats has no language of his own for this realm of experience*" (p. 174). Keats's mode is pictorial, and this mode "allows him to present the thesis of his dilemma, the ideality of the nightingale symbol, but not the antithesis, the world of common experience, which is the substance of stanza three. . . . The climax contains a little less than the full situation; it reaches us a little too simplified" (p. 176).

My dissent can be summarized in the counterassertion that, with certain inevitable reservations, the privation is as vividly realized as is the ideal plenitude. The personifications of age, youth, beauty, and love are vitalized by their contexts; they are comparable to "Veiled Melancholy" in "her sovran shrine" in the *Ode on Melancholy*, and the personifications of *To Autumn*. The particulars transform the abstractions, which are themselves explicable as necessary economies in a broadly typical account. (Any sort of detailed and documented realism would be unthinkable.) Time and the pressure of actuality, Mr. Tate to the contrary, are dramatized in parallelism, repetition, and progression. "The weariness, the fever, and the fret"; "a few, sad, last grey hairs"; "grows pale, and spectre-thin, and dies"; here is the process of tedium, time, and decay; here is the very movement of the meaning. The four-fold repetition of "where" is a further reinforcement, with its rhetorical suggestion of rising emotion to counterbalance the falling series of time. The stanza, one may well assert, has an intensity equal to its antithesis of the imaginative ideal, as Douglas Bush has remarked in his persuasive argument that the real theme of Keats's six great odes is the sadness of mutability.[3] It has also, what Professor Bush failed to point out, an energy of thought and a complex suavity which is best indicated in the last two lines—an effect in which personification plays a considerable part.

One grows uncomfortably aware of the limits of explication upon such an issue. I cannot say what shadows of Tom Keats and Fanny Brawne may haunt my reading of stanza 3, nor what reverberations from that old-fashioned doctrine of sincerity. One is left, at any rate, with a feeling that objective analysis goes only halfway—an avowal the humility of which is perhaps damaged by the fact that I wish to hit Mr. Tate with it more than myself. Assuming that Keats is a pictorial poet, he finds stanza 3 inadequately pictorial. Here he is pushing a metaphor too far. The *Nightingale* does not seem a notably pictorial poem; in it the associations of objects are much more important than their outlines.

The crucial issue, however, is the conception of unity implied by Mr. Tate's criticism. What can properly be asked of a poem? The first consideration in the *Nightingale* ode is the imaginative experience of the ideal. Different elements come into the picture, but there is at bottom one emphasis only. The objection to stanza 3 comes from very interesting assumptions about the nature of poetic unity, wholeness, and the reconciliation of opposites, which should be examined.

According to these assumptions unity is less important than wholeness, which in turn might be defined as an ideal reconciliation of all possible opposites. I argue against them that no poem is whole in this sense, or finally in any but its own terms. No poem contains all modes of experience, or even two experiences or ideas projected with equal force. The reconciliation of equal opposites is a theoretical, not an actual process; it would be colorless, odorless, tasteless, faceless. All logical opposites stand to each other in a dual relationship. They are first conceived as equals in that they are opposed; but they then arrange themselves in varying relations of inequality. Imagination can be reconciled to reason as the whole of which reason is a part; or the relation may be one of predominance, in which some elements of the weaker opposite are sacrificed to bring it into line—as a conservative will argue that he has incorporated the best features of progressivism into his conservative system. Opposites can be reconciled through related qualities of feeling, or simply by having common attributes. In a loose sense they may be said to be reconciled through the fact that they coexist, as in the romantic assumption that reality is One. The concept of the reconciliation of opposites, then, covers many processes, none of which corresponds precisely with the theoretical ideal. And none of these processes can be dismissed as in itself incomplete or dishonest.

If a poem, then, is thought of as a logical argument (which is to use an imperfect metaphor), the poet is under no obligation to do literal justice to both sides of the question, which would in any event be impossible. He does enough if he makes his argument interesting. If he also shows an awareness of other opinions, so much the better. If he seems crucially engaged with his problem we permit him to be a little unceremonious. In the *Nightingale* Keats is both interesting and as well-mannered as a man need be who is expressing his convictions. He is affirming the value of the ideal, and this is the primary fact. He is also paying due tribute to the power of the actual, and this is an important but secondary consideration. The stress of the poem lies in the conflict of value and power. Keats is at once agonized and amused at the inescapable discrepancy between them. He reconciles them by a prior imaginative acceptance of the unity of experience, by means of which he invests them with a common extremity and intensity of feeling. He need not give equal attention to both, for the actual can take care of itself; it is the frail ideal which requires bolstering.

The manner of Keats's reconciliation of opposites appears in stanza 4:

Not charioted by Bacchus and his pards,
But on the viewless wings of Poesy.

This rejection is only ostensible. Like Coleridge, and as W. H. Auden has remarked about the romantics in general, Keats prefers "both . . . and" to "either . . . or." The "draught of vintage" is not cancelled by, but combined with the vision in the forest, which deepens rather than discards the suggestions of "flora and the country green." The intuitive speed of imagination is dramatized by "already with thee!" The forest scene is romantically picturesque without being really pictorial: one does not visualize it, but its composition is describable in visual metaphor. Its unity is a matter of blending, with objects softened and distanced by the veil of darkness, which itself shades off into moonlight filtered through forest leaves. The moonlight, a symbol of imagination, intermingling with darkness evokes the enchantment of mystery, the wondrous secret just out of reach. After thus using suggestion Keats goes on to specification, much as he has done with "Bacchus and his pards." The imagery is particular and sensuous, but not highly visual. Hawthorne, eglantine, violets, and musk rose are important chiefly for their pastoral associations.

In the total effect sensations are blended in a soft and complex unity. Odor merges with touch and kinesthetic strain in "what soft incense hangs upon the boughs." "The grass, the

thicket, and the fruit tree wild" have tactual and plastic qualities. The "fast fading violets" are invested with organic sensation through empathy by being "covered up in leaves," and the
associations of the musk rose include taste and sound. As in
stanza 2 the theme is fulness, but with an added poignance and
complexity from the introduction of darkness and death. The
generous fertility of nature is inseparable from the grave, the
height demands its complement in depth, and intensest life
turns imperceptibly to its opposite.

The death theme, however, may easily be made too much
of. The embalmed darkness and fast fading violets certainly
suggest it, but the imaginative escape of stanza 4 is less into
death (or the womb) than into an ideal nature. The death of
stanza 5 is, indeed, a reasonable inference from the experience
of the forest. As freedom, ease, intensity, plenitude, and consummation the two are one. Death is easeful and rich, it is associated
with the nightingale's song in lavishness of giving. "To cease
upon the midnight" is in one respect the same as "pouring forth
thy soul abroad." In each is an outpouring, and a release from
the prisoning self. This imaginative acceptance of death is not,
however, unreserved. "I have been *half* in love with easeful
Death" and "Now more than ever seems it rich to die" are
measured statements. The acceptance, in fact, includes the res-
ervation, since it is an acceptance of the limits as well as the
freedoms of this death:

Still wouldst thou sing, and I have ears in vain—
To thy high requiem become a sod.

Momentarily death has identified Keats with the nightingale,
but only momentarily. Its meaning shifts from the most heightened consciousness to blank oblivion, and what seemed pure
spirit is sheer inert mass.

In another swift transition the death theme turns to a basis
for the immortality of the nightingale: a shift which restresses
both the identification and the withdrawal from the identifica-

tion. We are probably no longer greatly troubled by the objection seen by Robert Bridges, that the bird is obviously *not* immortal.[4]

H. W. Garrod has remarked that the nightingale commences as a particular bird, but is imaginatively transformed to a myth in such phrases as "light-winged Dryad of the trees."[5] The objection has also been met by the suggestion that Keats is thinking of the species, not the individual nightingale. Both of these solutions seem provisionally true; a little further on I wish to comment on the mortal-immortal difficulty as it is peculiar to Keats's imagination. In stanza 7, at any rate, the bird is a universal and undying voice: the voice of nature, of imaginative sympathy, and therefore of an ideal romantic poetry, infinitely powerful and profuse (compare the "profuse strains of unpremeditated art" of Shelley's *Skylark*, and the "music loud and long" of *Kubla Khan*). As sympathy it resolves all differences into the main fact of what Hawthorne has called the magnetic chain of humanity. It speaks to high and low; it comforts the human homesickness of Ruth and frees her from bitter isolation; and equally it opens the casements of the remote and magical. Lines 65–70 perhaps contain the two kinds of romanticism which Coleridge differentiated in Chapter 14 of *Biographia Literaria:* but the domestic and the exotic varieties are linked by their common purpose of fusing the usual with the strange. Ruth is distanced and framed by time and rich association, but in relation to the magic casements she is homely and familiar.

These magic casements are the apex and the climax of the imaginative experience. They are deliberately towering and frail, dramatizing the value, the gallantry, and precariousness of the romantic imagination at its height. They are connected with the actual by defying it, by their affirmation that what the mind can imagine is beauty and truth, an experience to be prized all the more for its brevity. The different senses of "forlorn," upon which Mr. Brooks has acutely commented, relate the passage to Ruth as well as to the final stanza, which returns to common earth. Ruth is forlorn in her loneliness. The faery lands are pleasurably forlorn in a remoteness which is really the condition of their value. "Forlorn" is like a bell which tolls the death of the imagination.

Stanza 8, despite the suddenness of the transition, is nevertheless a soft and quiet withdrawal from the heights. "The fancy cannot cheat so well / As she is famed to do" is not a rejection of imagination, but part of the total experience. The diction is unobtrusively lowered, to give an effect of half-humorous ruefulness. The inner movement of the conclusion is objectified in the gradual fading of the song, "Past the near meadows, over the still stream, / Up the hillside," in a perfect fusion of outward setting with mental experience. I am unable to see deep significance in the fact that the bird is now "buried deep / In the next valley-glade," but it would seem that it works like Wordsworth's

But there's a tree, of many, one,
A single field which I have looked upon,
Both of them speak of something that is gone,

by emphasizing a difference in sameness. The line recalls the "embalmed darkness" of the forest dim, and thus realizes the gulf between the earlier participation and the final withdrawal.

Was it a vision, or a waking dream?
Fled is that music:—do I wake or sleep?

These questions are objective in that they portray rather than abstract from Keats's state of mind. Like the beginning of the poem they suggest a prostrating reaction to an experience too powerful to be mastered, while as questions they also express an attempt to control and to understand it. Intellectually they raise a vital issue of romanticism, which might be underlined by remembering that Keats's original draft ran, "Was it a vision *real* or waking dream?"[6] It is the problem of the truth of imagination, which adds a further tension to the various stresses of actual and ideal. "I am certain," wrote Keats, "of nothing but of the holiness of the heart's affections, and the truth of imagination. What the imagination seizes as beauty must be truth."[7] Which was the dream, and which the reality? Which was the true, the peak or the plain, the rare or the commonplace, the ideal of permanence or the fact of change?

The answer concerns our problem of the reconciliation of opposites. The imaginative ideal is in a sense more true because it is more valuable, and the *Ode to a Nightingale* celebrates the poetic imagination. As it opposes the ideal to the actual, imagination against commonsense reason, imagination and ideal still predominate. They stand to their opposites as high against low, apex against base, action against reaction. Ideal and actual meet only as extremes, joined in the circle of experience. But the full power of the poem comes from adding the deadly question, is not the worse the true, the better illusion? Should we not change the meaning of truth?

The *Ode to a Nightingale* contains the highest, the fullest, the most intense, the most valuable mental experience which Keats can imagine. This is its center, this the basis of its unity. Within this unity, however, is a complex of feeling and thought which moves in alternate swellings and subsidences, a series of waves, each with its attendant trough. These waves are not of equal height; they rise gradually to a climax in stanza 7, and the rise subsides in the conclusion. Marshall McLuhan has suggested the musical organization of the fugue to define the structures of Keats's odes.[8] Most ambitious romantic poems of inner experience, indeed, offer wide variety of mood, with sudden and dramatic transitions. The *Ode on Intimations of Immortality*, with its organ-like swellings and sinkings, and its abrupt and effective changes of direction, is similar to the *Nightingale* in organization. Both make central affirmations, and both make these affirmations interesting by providing a controlled complexity of movement based upon a crucial suspense. Keats concludes with a question and Wordsworth with an answer, of course, but then Wordsworth knew more answers than Keats.

I have repeatedly made use of the metaphors of wholeness and intensity in this essay. In explication they are radically metaphors, I believe, rather than complete concepts. The theory of wholeness earlier imputed to Mr. Tate is equivalent to the metaphysical wit described by Eliot, the inclusive poetry of Richards, the ironic poetry of Brooks and Warren, and the poetry of knowledge adumbrated by John Crowe Ransom in *The World's Body*, which is not the poetry of children, nor of the heart's desire, but of the fallen mind, "since ours too are fallen." Such poetry is to be armed at all points, invulnerable to irony. Nothing can be objected to it, for it has foreseen all objections. It is a poetry of wholeness in that it has synthesized all conceivable arguments and attitudes. It follows that its conception of synthesis emphasizes the number and the diversity of the elements to be synthesized, and gives correspondingly less attention to the synthesizing agent. A poem constructed on this theory would emphasize difficulties and contradictions, discords and roughness, and only on inspection should its unity emerge, ideally the more satisfying because it has been struggled for.

Keats's notion of wholeness has the same elements as the modern, but with a different order and emphasis. "The excellence of every art is its intensity, capable of making all disagreeables evaporate, from their being in close relationship with Beauty and Truth."[9] Here the agent of synthesis comes first, the unity and the harmony, not the complexity and the discordance. The "disagreeables" must be attended to, but Keats is confident that they can be "evaporated" in intensity. The difference in emphasis might be illustrated in Tate's comments on Longinus' famous account of Sappho's ode. In Longinus Mr. Tate sees an early exponent of the reconciliation of opposites, who is using wholeness and complexity as his criteria of excellence.[10] A romantic, however, would probably settle first upon the passion which has unified the complexity, and would then interest himself in Longinus' remarks about the principle of selection in the poem. Sappho does not give everything, but only a selected part of the whole. The ode is an essence, not an imitation of reality. The details are chosen for the greatest intensity of concentration, with the irrelevant and trivial excluded.

Intense concentration of effect in Keats, the loading every rift with ore, is a way of obtaining profusion, as the *Nightingale* itself demonstrates. F. R. Leavis has said that "one remembers the poem both as recording, and as being for the reader, an indulgence."[11] I find Mr. Leavis too austere, but he points out a quality which Keats plainly sought for. His profusion and prodigality is, however, modified by a principle of sobriety. He has recorded both the profusion and its attendant restraint:

1st. I think poetry should surprise by a fine excess, and not by singularity; it should strike the reader as a wording of his own highest thoughts, and appear almost as a remembrance.
2nd. Its touches of beauty should never be halfway, thereby making the reader breathless, instead of content. The rise, the progress, the setting of Imagery should, like the sun, come natural to him, shine over him, and set soberly, although in magnificence, leaving him in the luxury of twilight. . . . Another axiom—That if poetry comes not as naturally as the leaves to a tree, it had better not come at all.[12]

This passage can be taken, I think, to represent the artistic purposes of the *Nightingale*. Wholeness, intensity, and naturalness are its appropriate standards. Nature is, indeed, the real norm—the physical face of nature, nature as it appears to the romantic imagination—and wholeness and intensity are attributes of nature, as are freedom, ease, spontaneity, harmony, and sobriety. Imagined as the Golden Age of Flora and the country green, and more fully as the forest of the nightingale, it becomes first the bird, the voice of nature; then the ideal poet; and finally the ideal itself. This nature is the antithesis of the privative actual in stanza 3.

The nature of the *Nightingale* is particular, since it conforms to its dramatic situation. The rich darkness of the forest is peculiar to the poem, not literally entire and universal. The poet uses his donnée, and no extension of his symbols will transcend its limits. Given his particular and concrete nature, Keats infers from it peace, fulfilment, and ideal freedom. His apprehension of nature is characteristically romantic but peculiarly his own in its sensuous immediacy. While he feels the romantic impulsion toward an overarching and ideal unity, in him the sensuous real is inseparable from its ideal opposite. It is as if for Keats the primary and secondary imaginations of Coleridge were one, and the process of "dissolving, diffusing, dissipating, in order to recreate" unnecessary to him. To his apprehension physical nature is immediately absolute and permanent. In the *Nightingale*, as in *To Autumn*, he arrests change in mid-motion by contemplation apotheosized, which fixes the temporal object within a timeless frame. And thus the immortality of the nightingale; it is a question of focus. Nature is always dying but always alive, forever changing but always the same. With the nightingale Keats fixes his imagination upon sameness and life.

The standard of nature involves effects of spontaneity and artlessness which sometimes confuse us into suspecting that the poet is confusing his art with reality. The romantics have laid themselves open to this misconstruction, but it is nevertheless a great mistake to take their artistic imitations for experience in the raw. The *Nightingale* imitates spontaneity without being spontaneous. Its opening lines, for example, are calculated to disarm judgment by a show of unrehearsed feeling. These lines are, however, a classic instance of Keats's technique. The repeated suggestions in "as though of hemlock I had drunk," "emptied some dull opiate to the drains," and "Lethe-wards had sunk," with their undersong of assonance, are obviously more than coincidental.

The transitional links of the poem are also at first sight spontaneous and merely associational. They are too invariably happy, however, to be literally unpremeditated. H. W. Garrod has asserted that the transitions of the *Nightingale* are governed by Keats's intoxication with his own words. "The infection of his own accidents of style, if I may so call them, compels the direction of thought; the rhythm and words together determine the stanza which comes next."[13] One wonders what or who

113

determines the rhythm and words. More recently Albert Guérard, Jr., viewing the *Nightingale* as a poem which consummately expresses the universal impulse toward submersion of consciousness, has said that this impulse is a "longing not for art but a free reverie of any kind. The form of the poem is that of progression by association, so that the movement of feeling is at the mercy of words evoked by chance, such words as *fade* and *forlorn*, the very word which like a bell tolls the dreamer back to his sole self."[14] This passage occurs in an interesting and a favorable account of the poem. Mr. Guérard, like Garrod, admires Keats. Nevertheless, "longing not for art but a free reverie of any kind," and "the movement of the feeling is at the mercy of words evoked by chance" constitute damaging charges, indicting the *Ode* for bad art and low-grade mental activity. Such charges against romantic poems have become rather frequent since Babbitt reigned. A romantic critic still has trouble answering them, however, because their assumptions are strange to him. One is always dismayed to find what he had happily taken for a virtue suddenly and persuasively attacked as one of the lower forms of vice.

I will nevertheless venture some suggestions on the specific problem of associational transitions like "fade away" and "forlorn." To adopt Mr. McLuhan's musical analogy, they are motifs woven into a varied musical pattern. Dramatically they are important in objectifying the theme in a word, revealing instantaneously the central stress of the poem. They work like Wordsworth's tree, which focuses the problem of his ode, "Where is it now, the glory and the dream?" in a single concrete image. So "fade away" and "forlorn" dramatize sharply the two states of mind in the poem. Why they should be said to control the movement of the feeling is not clear to me; they appear only to *indicate* the movement, as patches of foam on the tops of the swells.

It is easy to make nonsense of the romantic aesthetic of nature by noticing only its major term, and omitting its elaborate qualifications. Coleridge gives its true emphasis, I think, in describing poetic imagination as the power which "while it blends and harmonizes the natural and the artificial, still subordinates art to nature, the manner to the matter; and our admiration of the poet to our sympathy with the poetry."[15] The natural must be blended with the artificial; art is to be subordinated, not extinguished. In this context art is to be understood as the appearance of art, as it strikes the eye of the beholder; Coleridge is not establishing a quota on the art which can actually go into the poem.

10

Beauty and Truth
John Middleton Murry on Keats

My impression is that Murry is not talked about much just now among Keats scholars. I recollect, however, the late C. D. Thorpe, himself the author of an epoch-making interpretation of Keats's poetry, paying tribute to Murry's influence in getting people to take Keats seriously as a thinker. More recently I have been interested to hear a respected student of English romanticism declare that Murry is the best of all critics of Keats—a judgment that may be a straw in the wind. It is not to my purpose to discuss the progress of Keats scholarship in general. It is probable, however, that many of Murry's contributions have been assimilated and their source forgotten—a thoroughly usual circumstance; and also that scholars with a reputation of sobriety to maintain prefer to stay away from him. Murry in an apocalyptic mood is a mighty heady draught, capable of reminding us, say, of Sir Max Beerbohm parodying Frank Harris on Shakespeare. Thus, I think, his fine insights are liable to be lost in their own profusion, and drowned in the rush of his eloquence.

116

His actual achievement is very substantial indeed.[1] In his *Keats and Shakespeare* he succeeds in conceiving of a unique and autonomous poetic mode or thought, which to my mind is all-important. Writing in the 1920s, he does so without resorting to or being forced into a theory of myth to explain poetry, which is all to the good. (He may have been forced into biography instead, which is not so good.) As a consequence Murry is able to show in Keats a uniquely poetical and concrete way of thinking, and correspondingly to demonstrate an ultimate fusion of beauty and truth (his primary theme) as its result. The beauty-truth problem pervades his *Keats and Shakespeare* and his later Keats studies as well. Murry solves the problem, too, in his own terms and to his own satisfaction, with entire self-consistency. Whether the solution is satisfying to everybody is of course a more difficult question.

The beauty-truth equation leads in turn to a notion that we owe substantially to Murry, though not uniquely, since it is to be found in early critics such as Colvin and A. C. Bradley. That is, that Keats achieved a unique state of acceptance, such as is expressed in the "ripeness is all" of *King Lear*, and that this acceptance ("Beauty is Truth, Truth Beauty") is most consummately and fully embodied in the last great ode, *To Autumn*, with its resolution of fertility and death in harmony ("Think not of them, thou hast thy music too"). Again, it seems to me that by his grasp of Keats's poetic thought, expanded into a theory of poetic thought in general, Murry is able to convey as has no other critic since A. C. Bradley the imaginative unity of sensation and idealism in Keats. In particular he is successfully romantic and magnanimous in his treatment of such terms as "sensation" and "speculation" in Keats.[2] He is subtle in comprehending the complex inclusiveness of Keats's meanings.

Murry anticipated, and is no doubt to a large degree responsible, for the widespread belief among some interpreters that Keats would have turned to the drama if he had lived, as the ideal form for his Shakespearean genius for "negative capability." Bernice Slote has most fully projected the idea in her *Keats and the Dramatic Principle*. It is not wholly a digression from

Murry, who is our theme, to discuss this theory for a little. Unquestionably Keats aspired to be a dramatist, as similar to Shakespeare as he could manage to be. He said wonderful things in his letters about Shakespeare, about dramatic character, and about his own bent for dramatic objectivity. He enjoyed the stage and saw as many plays as he could. Yet there is simply no concrete evidence that he could have produced or perhaps would have deeply wanted to commit himself to the real thing. His *King Otho*, written under impossible conditions, is inconclusive. Miss Slote has managed a remarkable tour de force by reconstructing his *Lamia* as a play, with descriptions turned into stage directions, but the fact remains that *Lamia* is a narrative poem. Keats's last considerable work is his recast of the unfinished epic *Hyperion* into *The Fall of Hyperion*, and what he did to it in his new *Induction* was to turn it into an allegory, sui generis but with resemblances to Spenser, and yet further back to the medieval dream vision convention.

Furthermore, the very affinity with Shakespeare that is Murry's first presumption might well have been disastrous for Keats as a practising dramatist. We well know that Shakespearean blank verse and its associations proved an impossible barrier to nineteenth-century efforts at poetic drama. Could Keats have broken the barrier, could he have captured the essential Shakespeare and, as no one else could do, thrown off the dead weight of the superficial form of the Shakespearean language and structure? It would take great faith to suppose it.

Murry too little regards here the mere matter of the genre itself; and this is a fit occasion to comment upon his weaknesses as a critic of Keats. These are weaknesses, it will be understood, from my point of view, because I think differently about the issues. In itself his Keats criticism is remarkably self-consistent, and this consistency is a main source for its unusual vitality. "It is no part of the purpose of this book" (*Keats and Shakespeare*, p. 129), he says, "to appreciate Keats' poems objectively as poetry; its concern is solely to elucidate the deep and natural movement of the poet's soul which underlies them." Fair warning, and perhaps exculpation; but it is not wholly acceptable. I do not insist that Keats's poems be detached from Keats, but they ought at least to be allowed out now and then for an airing. Besides it is Murry's Keats to whom they are thus bound. One result is the identification of Keats with his characters; with the young Apollo of his *Hyperion*, for instance. "This is no appeal of an immortal: Apollo is no God. He is none other than the mortal Keats; and he is the mortal Keats at one period of his life and no other. This 'isle' that he longs to flee from is this earth of ours; his agonized appeal is but a premonitory echo of the agonized appeal in the *Ode to a Nightingale*" (*Keats and Shakespeare*, p. 90).

Setting aside the fact that there is no "agonized appeal" in the *Ode to a Nightingale*, Apollo is not a mortal in any sense that is true to *Hyperion*. Keats has the technical problem that the Titan Hyperion is still in power, which gives him a difficulty of portrayal. But this does not make Apollo a mortal. Further it hems him in too tightly within Murry's sense of Keats's chronological development ("Keats at one period of his life and no other"), and it makes the whole mythological "machinery" of *Hyperion* meaningless. Thus Madeline and Lamia are both Fanny Brawne—and if one complains, Murry scoffs at the complaint for literal-mindedness.[3] Like Amy Lowell, Murry is strongly inclined to run away with Keats, meanwhile indignantly fending off anyone else who "tries to get into the act." Intending, as he does, "to elucidate the deep and natural movement of the poet's soul," he also intends to be its sole custodian. Interestingly, after praising the first volume of her massive biography of Keats he condemned the second, one suspects primarily because Miss Lowell attempted to prove that *The Fall of Hyperion* was written earlier than *Hyperion*, a notion which suited her conception of Keats's development extremely well, but played havoc with Murry's. His refutation of her arguments (*Keats and Shakespeare*, pp. 242–248) has been generally accepted as correct. In a similar instance Murry was greatly exercised at Robert Gittings's introduction of Mrs. Isabella Jones as a serious rival of Fanny Brawne in Keats's affections, and the inspiration for *The Eve of St. Agnes*. His rebuttal, "Keats and Isabella Jones"

(*Keats*, pp. 104–144), is to my mind entirely in the right, and his analysis of Gittings's readings in Keats's poetry is devastating.

I shall now summarize Murry's position on Keats as I understand it, returning to his basic claims for poetry, or rather for the poetic process. He commenced, he says, with "the history of the human soul since the Renaissance," which is essentially "the history of the most remarkable and individual human souls since the Renaissance" (*Keats and Shakespeare*, p. 1). These souls are the poets. "To know a work of literature is to know the soul of the man who created it, and who created it in order that his soul should be known. . . . The writer's soul is that which moves our souls" (ibid., p. 3). Intending, as Murry says, to use Shakespeare, "himself verily 'the prophetic soul of the wide world dreaming of things to come,' " he found him too difficult to present.

I had gradually grown accustomed to a kind of thinking which is not the ordinary kind of thinking at all; I had formed the habit first of making certain translations between poetic thought and rational thought, and then of discarding these translations altogether; I had come to assume a whole system of correspondences between purely poetic imagery and the steps of discursive thinking—correspondences, I insist, and not equivalences—which I could not reasonably require other minds to assume without a demonstration which to be convincing must not be incidental. . . . I saw that my one chance of making intelligible these slowly formed convictions of mine concerning Shakespeare was to use the greatest of his successors, John Keats, as though he were a mediator between the normal consciousness of men and the pure poetic consciousness in which form alone Shakespeare remains to us. (pp. 3–4)

Murry quickly decided—like Coleridge on Shakespeare—that Keats is beyond the reach of judicial criticism. "The thing that Keats actually was is infinitely more perfect than any perfection we can invent for him. The proper attitude of criticism toward Keats is one of complete humility" (p. 5).

Murry is conceiving the soul as the totality of man, the mind and heart as parts of him, to be reconciled and subsumed within the larger conception. The soul is integral, synthetic. The poet ("in ideal perfection," as Coleridge says), is the great historian of the soul, the true psychologist, the prophet, the seer. The terms are almost interchangeable. Thus Murry remarks that

people who should know better have a strange habit of talking as though psychology were a new invention of the nineteenth century, because the word and the study came into vogue at that time. Someday they may awake to the simple fact that literary creators like Shakespeare and Keats had forgotten more psychology than the most advanced psycho-analyst ever knew. Psychology is either true knowledge concerning the spiritual nature of man or it is moonshine and abracadabra: perhaps, when we are a little nearer the millennium, the psychologists will take it into their heads to go for the elements of their science to the past-masters of it—those creative writers whose productions are recognized by the consensus of generations to be "just representations of human nature." (p. 230)

So he says in the 1920s. Since then psychology has taken his advice with a vengeance, but in a fashion that Murry neither anticipated nor desired. Much later, talking of the possibility of classifying "feeling-types" of men of imaginative genius, he commented, "Dr. Jung in his suggestive book, *Psychological Types*, has boldly, but perhaps prematurely, attempted a detailed classification. But he has, at least, conclusively established that 'scientific' psychology—in the peculiarly modern sense of reductive psychology—is useless in this realm; by its assumptions it abolishes the very phenomena to be studied." Murry would have had the psychologist go to the poet as a disciple to a master, not as a surgeon to an autopsy.

The poet is the prophet and seer, and poetry is religion or scripture—or since Murry's religion is without objective dogma, it may be better to put it that religion becomes essential poetry. The poet's insight is intuitive and inward; such souls as Shakespeare and Keats transcend the self by intense self-contemplation. Murry intends to be an inward biographer of the soul, taking his cue, perhaps, from Keats's famous remark that Shakespeare's life was a continual allegory, with his works the comment upon it. Thus the man and his works are essentially the same, his poetry the expression of his deepest nature.

Keats and Shakespeare are perfectly integrated souls; unlike most men, they were not dominated by the mere reason, which is no more than an outward incrustation upon human nature. They have no trace of dogmatism, they do not force conclusions, they have the ability to love both good and ill alike. In their ultimate insight they become even as gods, who know and pass beyond the mortal bars. So, for Keats, light and shade become one, aesthetically a harmony and morally a final revelation.

This is a key-phrase in his conception of poetry. The connection appears plainly in his description of the Poetic Character. "It enjoys light and shade . . . it does no harm from its relish of the dark side of things any more than from its taste for the bright one, because they both end in speculation."

He applies it in his remarks on *Paradise Lost*.

The light and shade—the sort of black brightness—the ebon diamonding—the Ethiop Immortality—the sorrow, the pain, the sad-sweet Melody—the Phalanges [Phalanxes?] of Spirits so depressed as to be "uplifted beyond hope"—the short mitigation of Misery—the thousand Melancholies and Magnificences of this page—leaves no room for anything to be said but "so it is."[4]

Keats, then, reconciles light and shade, beauty and truth. He does not need to reason and learn in the ordinary sense, discursively. He makes no distinction between inner and outer, his thought is concrete and poetic, and this is the highest consciousness and insight. Keats and Shakespeare are essentially Christian, and in the best sense catholic.

I should say that Shakespeare and Keats were of the catholic feeling-type and Milton was of the protestant feeling-type; and that they were very pure examples of their type. . . . If I am required to describe the catholic type, at a high level I should say it is much more conscious than the protestant type of the mystery of existence, and in particular of the mystery of suffering; and much more conscious of the limitations of the human reason. This, I should say, derived from a different quality of primary experience, which comes to the catholic nature immediate, warm, and perplexing.[5]

Murry's mode of thought, or the central structure from which he consistently proceeds, is essentially organic and romantic. As such I sympathize with it, and his consistent application of his central insight endows his Keats criticism with luminous vitality. He unmistakably "has something there." Yet, and in part for the very reason that I myself would like to be as romantic and organic as I think is reasonable, I do not think his criticism entirely serviceable to the good cause. It is too close to absolute monism, and thus to monotony. It is this habit of thought, probably, that impels him into irritating repetitions and rhetorical exhortations. Like some other romantics, he knows and is obsessed with one great truth—oneness—and without quite realizing it he is always striking inwards at it, though from many angles and directions. Organicism, in prose discourse at least, must come to terms with discursive thought, with dualism, with the outer. Murry does not give the difficulties to be faced, the oppositions to be reconciled, enough provisional reality to convince us that he has really faced them, and has genuinely accomplished the romantic mission. I could not accept Keats's poetry, for example, as the expression of Keats's soul—which in a sense it certainly must be—unless I had first detached it thoroughly from Keats for examination.

11

Weird Mockery
An Element of Hawthorne's Style

In the 1851 Preface to *Twice-Told Tales* Hawthorne remarks on "the coolness of a meditative habit, which diffuses itself through the feeling and observation of every sketch." He goes on to say, however, that "they have none of the abstruseness of idea, or obscurity of expression, which mark the written communications of a solitary mind with itself. They never need translation. It is, in fact, the style of a man of society." He concludes, "This statement of apparently opposite peculiarities leads us to a perception of what the sketches truly are. They are not the talk of a secluded man with his own mind and heart . . . , but his attempts, and very imperfectly successful ones, to open an intercourse with the world."

Hawthorne is, then, quite willing to accept the responsibility that was laid upon writers of English and American fiction from the time of Henry Fielding to Henry James. The author must in general explain himself, introduce, act as master of ceremonies, according to the best of his abilities charm the reader, himself abstracted and personified as "The Gentle Reader." In his long sketch *Main-Street*, which covers two centuries of Salem history, Hawthorne employs the persona of a showman who is exhibiting a "moving panorama," and who must comment, give proper emphasis, and sometimes defend against unsympathetic members of the audience. He is thoroughly conscious of an audience, although he must at times grope for its identity or even its existence. In Hawthorne's particular case, he is perhaps more willing to assume the obligations and self-renunciations of the urbane "man of society" as an author than as a person. Or, it might be said, as a shy and rather unmalleable man he is extremely conscious of his own social deficiencies, and tries to compensate for them when he is protected by the aesthetic (and safe) distance of his fiction. We may remember Emerson's complaint of him, that never being able to get much out of Hawthorne he talked too much himself, which only deepened Hawthorne's reserve; and we have Henry James Sr.'s description of him at a banquet of the Saturday Club. Sitting at table, he reminded James of "a pickpocket between two detectives."

He is probably more communicative as a writer than he was as a man. Yet his phrase, "the style of a man in society," contains its own reserves and distances along with its implied obligations. Towards the end of the charming sketch that introduces *Mosses from an Old Manse* to the reader (to whom he refers as "Mine honored reader"), he reflects,

How little have I told! and of that little, how almost nothing is even tinctured with any quality that makes it exclusively my own! Has the reader gone wandering, hand in hand with me, through the inner passages of my being? and have we groped together into all its chambers and examined their treasures or their rubbish? Not so. We have been standing on the greensward, but just within the cavern's mouth, where the common sunshine is free to penetrate, and where every footstep is therefore free to come. I have appealed to no sentiment or sensibilities save such as are diffused among us all. So far as I am a man of really individual attributes I veil my face.

We should expect, then, from Hawthorne's work, a certain generality of style, a courteous regard for his imagined reader, which involves from mutual respect an assumption of frankness and ease along with an equally well-intentioned reticence. If what Hawthorne says is a full account of his fiction, we should need to go no further; there is of course much more to be said. But we must allow for a painstaking clarity of exposition and at the same time an unyielding reticence. The interposition of the graceful "man of society" causes the fiction itself to stand quite far back, and "the coolness of a meditative habit" is a phrase that can be given a contemporary meaning: Hawthorne inveterately "keeps his cool." The result is a kind of detachment that makes his meaning hard to penetrate, despite his polite authorial comment upon it.

What I am preparing to say about Hawthorne's *style* may be clarified a little by resorting to what I. A. Richards said some time ago about *tone* as the attitude of a speaker to his listener. "The tone of his utterance reflects his awareness of this relation, his sense of how he stands towards those he is addressing." "Indeed, many of the secrets of 'style' could, I believe, be shown to be matters of tone, of the perfect recognition of the writer's relation to the reader in view of what is being said and their joint feelings about it." Tone is a question of manners, and good tone involves proportion. Discussing Gray's *Elegy*, Richards declares that "by the tone in which a great writer handles these familiar things we can tell whether they have their due place in the whole fabric of his thought and feeling, and whether, therefore, he has the right to our attention. Good manners, fundamentally, are a reflection of our sense of proportion."[1] Hawthorne's awareness of tone is great, and his sense of proportion exquisite, although he is certainly not always dealing with familiar things. In his beauty, there is indeed "some *strangeness* in the proportions," but this comes from understatement and coolness rather than overstatement and excitement. He says what abstractedly may be regarded as some quite wonderful and terrible things, but he says them very calmly.

This calm led Henry James to believe that Hawthorne used

his Puritan heritage of gloom purely as a fanciful plaything. There is an important truth in this, although the man whose intelligence, as T. S. Eliot said, was too fine to be violated by ideas, may be reading something of himself into his older American colleague. This side of Hawthorne's case has never been put better than by James:

Nothing is more curious and interesting than this almost exclusively *imported* character of the sense of sin in Hawthorne's mind; it seems to exist there merely for an artistic or literary purpose. He had ample cognizance of the Puritan conscience; it was his natural heritage; it was reproduced in him; looking into his soul, he found it there. But his relation to it was only, as one may say, intellectual; it was not moral and theological. He played with it, and used it as a pigment; he treated it, as the metaphysicians say, objectively. He was not discomposed, disturbed, haunted by it, in the manner of its usual or regular victims, who had not the little postern door of fancy to slip through, to the other side of the wall. It was, indeed, to his imaginative vision, the great fact of man's nature; the light element that had been mingled with his own composition always clung to this rugged prominence of moral responsibility, like the mist that hovers about the mountain.

... To speak of Hawthorne, as M. Emile Montégut does, as a *romancier pessimiste*, seems to me very much beside the mark. He is no more a pessimist than an optimist, though he is certainly not much of either. He does not pretend to conclude, or to have a philosophy of human nature; indeed, I should even say that at bottom he does not take human nature as hard as he may seem to do. "His bitterness," says M. Montégut, "is without abatement, and his bad opinion of man is without compensation.... His little tales have the air of confessions which the soul makes to itself; they are so many little slaps which the author applies to our face." This, it seems to me, is to exaggerate almost immeasurably the reach of Hawthorne's relish of gloomy subjects. What pleased him in such subjects was their picturesqueness, their rich duskiness of colour, their chiaroscuro; but they were not the expression of a hopeless, or even of a predominantly melancholy, feeling about the human soul. Such at least is my own impression. He is to a considerable degree ironical—this is part of his charm—part even, one may say, of his brightness; but he is neither bitter nor cynical—he is rarely even what I should call tragical. There have certainly been story-tellers of a gayer and brighter spirit; there have been observers more humorous, more hilarious—though on the whole Hawthorne's observation has a smile in it oftener than may at first appear; but there has rarely been an observer more serene, less agitated by what he sees and less disposed to call things deeply into question.[2]

This urbane and complicated statement is on the whole decidedly approving. James has reservations about Hawthorne's art, which he is inclined to relegate to the fancy. He allots "Young Goodman Brown," of which we shall have more to say later, to the imagination, but of the tales in general he makes his famous observation that "allegory, to my sense, is quite one of the lighter exercises of the imagination." He strongly suggests, however, that Hawthorne's detachment is the detachment of art itself, and that it is beneficent. He is rescued, as it were, from the trap of an unnecessary and inappropriate involvement by an aesthetic gift and attitude that are at bottom sanative. "Hawthorne, of course, was exceptionally fortunate; he had his genius to help him." Let us notice, at any rate, that James emphasizes the *objectivity* of Hawthorne, and that he concedes his "relish of gloomy subjects," though "he played with" the dark Puritan conscience, "and used it as a pigment."

Anthony Trollope's perceptive account of *The Scarlet Letter* has some interesting resemblances to James's. Trollope is astonished at the relentless gloom of the book ("It is so terrible in its pictures of diseased human nature as to produce most questionable delight"), but like James he points out that Hawthorne stands far back from his subject. The author intends that in the last analysis the reader should sympathize with Hester Prynne, yet he "deals with her in a spirit of assumed hardness." As a further complication, however, Hawthorne satirizes his own ostensible hardness, as he also inveterately satirizes "the peculiar institutions of his own country." "Indeed," Trollope reflects, "there is never a page written by Hawthorne not tinged by satire." At the end of his critique he elaborates, after mildly suggesting that the ending of the book is all too pitiless.

But through all this intensity of suffering, through this blackness of narrative, there is ever running a vein of drollery. As Hawthorne himself says, "a lively sense of the humourous again stole in among the solemn phantoms of her thought." He is always laughing at something with his weird, mocking spirit. The very children when they see Hester in the streets are supposed to speak to her in this wise: "Behold, verily, there is the woman of the scarlet letter. Come, therefore, and let us fling mud at her." Of some religious book he says, "It must have been a work of vast ability in the somniferous school of literature." "We must not always talk in the market-place of what happens to us in the forest," says even the sad mother to her child. Through it all there is a touch of burlesque,—not as to the suffering of the sufferers, but as to the great question whether it signifies much in what way we suffer, whether by crushing sorrows or little stings. . . . In this way Hawthorne seems to ridicule the very woes which he expends himself in depicting.[3]

The "drollery," the "weird mocking," and the "burlesque" are perhaps not quite the same as the satire that Trollope had earlier noticed, since their objects are more comprehensive: he is talking here of a sort of cosmic irony. The two phenomena are nevertheless alike as regards Hawthorne's attitude toward his material, his "tone."

Trollope believes more fully than James in the reality of Hawthorne's gloom. I turn now to a still more earnest believer: Melville in his 1850 review of *Mosses from an Old Manse*. Melville is not certain how much Hawthorne's "blackness" may be simply an artistic effect—and this is, though to a lesser degree, an issue in Melville's own work. He is interested in the blackness as a reality and as a stimulating peculiarity of effect, but chiefly in its reality and universal meaning.

For spite of all the Indian-summer sunlight on the hither side of Hawthorne's soul, the other side—like the dark half of the physical sphere—is shrouded in a blackness, ten times black. But this darkness but gives more effect to the evermoving dawn, that for ever advances through it, and circumnavigates his world. Whether Hawthorne has simply availed himself of this mystical blackness as a means to the wondrous effects he makes it to produce in his lights and shades; or whether there really lurks in him, perhaps unknown to himself, a touch of Puritan gloom,—this, I cannot altogether tell. Certain it is, however, that this great power of blackness in him derives its force from its appeals to that Calvinistic sense of Innate Depravity and Original Sin, from whose visitations, in some shape or other, no deeply thinking mind is always and wholly free. For, in certain moods, no man can weigh this world without throwing in something, somehow like Original Sin, to strike the uneven balance. At all events, perhaps no writer has ever wielded this terrific thought with greater terror than this same harmless Hawthorne. Still more: this black conceit pervades him through and through. You may be witched by his sunlight,—transported by the bright gildings in the skies he builds over you; but there is the blackness of darkness beyond; and even his bright gildings but fringe and play upon the edges of thunder-clouds. In one word, the world is mistaken in this Nathaniel Hawthorne. . . . He is immeasurably deeper than the plummet of the mere critic. For it is not the brain that can test such a man; it is only the heart. You cannot come to know greatness by inspecting it; there is no glimpse to be caught of it, except by intuition; you need not ring it, you but touch it, and you find it gold.

Now, it is that blackness in Hawthorne, of which I have spoken, that so fixes and fascinates me.[4]

This great bravura-piece has been said to describe Melville himself better than Hawthorne: just as it was earlier remarked that James's criticism of Hawthorne was somewhat inclined to be Jamesian. All good criticism, however, to misapply Coleridge, is "the coalescence of a subject and an object"; with "coalescence" the operative word. Literal truths are beyond and beneath criticism, and what Melville sees in Hawthorne is really there, whether, to quote another thinker, Keats, "it existed before or not." He wonderfully catches Hawthorne's "effect," especially his delicate fragility in such a phrase as "the bright gildings in the skies he builds over you." And he is intensely valuable upon the contrast between what Hawthorne says (abstracted from his style) and his style or manner of saying it. In many respects at the opposite extreme from James, who denies that the essential Hawthorne is touched by his inherited vision of sin, he nevertheless finds the same tone as James in his author.

Believing as he does in the reality of Hawthorne's blackness, Melville finds wondrous profundity beneath the surface of "Young Goodman Brown," that simply-titled fable.

"Who in the name of thunder" (as the country-people say in this neighborhood), "who in the name of thunder, would anticipate any marvel in a piece entitled 'Young Goodman Brown'?" You would of course suppose that it was a simple little tale, intended as a supplement to "Goody Two Shoes." Whereas, it is as deep as Dante; nor can you finish it, without addressing the author in his own words—"It is yours to penetrate, in every bosom, the deep mystery of sin."[5]

"Young Goodman Brown" will serve as the principal text for the peculiarity of style and tone that I want to examine, with some heed also to another tale, "My Kinsman, Major Molineux." As we have seen, James, Trollope, and Melville all agree upon emphasizing the theme of sin in Hawthorne. James maintains that he plays with it and uses it as a pigment. Trollope is somewhat startled, in talking of *The Scarlet Letter*, by the "weird mockery" of Hawthorne's treatment of his theme. Melville, who is most interested in it, makes reference to Hawthorne's apparent harmlessness. I recur momentarily to James's remark, too, that "on the whole Hawthorne's observation has a smile in it oftener than may at first appear." Finally, I wish to appropriate to Hawthorne I. A. Richards's "awareness," "good manners," and "sense of proportion."

It may be difficult for me to keep my own sense of proportion, however, since in trying to define Hawthorne's tone I shall maintain that Hawthorne's two stories of sin are both jokes upon their protagonists, and that the manner of them is frequently ironic, and sometimes, as Trollope hints of *The Scarlet Letter*, sheer parody. These are admittedly half-truths only, which I shall try to keep in balance by adverting to Hawthorne's own balance and perfection of tone. It may be that the comedy of these tales is no more than the kind of distancing that has already been specified, or, in James's fine terms, a consummate aesthetic and moral strategy: "Hawthorne's way was the best;

for he contrived, by an exquisite process, to transmute this heavy moral burden into the very substance of the imagination, to make it evaporate in the light and charming fumes of artistic production."⁶

The joke on Young Goodman Brown is a tremendous deception, brought about with the aid of self-deception. I do not think, as David Levin has interestingly maintained, that Brown is deluded in the forest by "spectral evidence." He sees too little rather than too much: everything is more complicated than he supposes. And this effect is conveyed by a kind of understatement and pretense of naivety. There is a stroke of wit in the phrase "Faith, as the wife was aptly named," considering all that is implied by "aptly," as there is a little later on when Brown tells the devil that " 'Faith kept me back a while.' " The devil himself is a master of understatement:

"Well said, Goodman Brown! I have been as well acquainted with your family as with ever a one among the Puritans; and that's no trifle to say. I helped your grand-father, the constable, when he lashed the Quaker woman so smartly through the streets of Salem; and it was I that brought your father a pitch-pine knot, kindled at my own hearth, to set fire to an Indian village, in King Philip's war. They were my good friends, both; and many a pleasant walk have we had along this path, and returned merrily after midnight. I would fain be friends with you for their sake."

They have been, in fact, boon-companions, and these are pleasant reminiscences, with a mildly agreeable vigor in "lashed the Quaker woman so smartly," "a pitch-pine knot, kindled at my own hearth," and "returned merrily after midnight." But the devil's best effort in this vein comes later, at the forest ceremony where Brown and his Faith are waiting to be initiated into his dark congregation. He describes to them the reality of secret sin:

This night it shall be granted you to know their secret deeds: how hoary-bearded elders of the church have whispered wanton words to the young maidens of their households; how many a woman, eager for widow's weeds, has given her husband a drink at bedtime and let him sleep his last sleep in her bosom; how beardless youths have made haste to inherit their fathers' wealth; and how fair damsels—blush not, sweet ones—have dug little graves in the garden, and bidden me, the sole guest, to an infant's funeral.[7]

The difference between matter and manner is great, considering that the matter is lust, murder most foul, and possibly abortion. There is a ceremonious gallantry, along with an indulgent chiding, in "fair damsels—blush not, sweet ones." Girls will be girls, and a very entertaining circumstance it is, too.

It has often been noticed that Hawthorne is not mimetic and expressive in dialogue. Relatively speaking, his characters all talk alike. Closely observed, however, in "Young Goodman Brown" there are subtle differentiations, and the differences are functional. We have seen that the devil is perversely formal, courteous, ceremonious (to omit the occasions when he sounds like Milton's Satan). No one but Faith would say " 'A lone woman is troubled with such dreams and such thoughts that she's afeard of herself sometimes' "—cadence and diction are uniquely hers. Goodman Brown (the effect is very delicate, and I am afraid of overstating it) parodies himself and the Puritan state of mind. His diction is lightly archaic, a little unctuous. There is quaintness, simplicity, complacency, and unconscious hypocrisy in it all at once; he has (again, very lightly touched) the Puritan biblical sanctimoniousness, the relishing of phrases on the tongue.

"What, my sweet, pretty wife, dost thou doubt me already, and we but three months married?" "If it be as thou sayest . . . I marvel they never spoke of these matters; or, verily, I marvel not, seeing that the least rumor of the sort would have driven them from New England. We are a people of prayer, and good works to boot, and abide no such wickedness."

In both stories, understatement and suggestion at some point give way to tremendous laughter. Thus the devil cannot quite restrain himself at the moral spectacle of Young Goodman Brown: he "now burst into a fit of irrepressible mirth, shaking himself so violently that his snake-like staff actually seemed to wriggle in sympathy.... 'Ha! ha! ha!' shouted he again and again...." In the forest the unhappy Brown is made aware of his Faith by "a scream, drowned immediately in a louder murmur of voices, fading into far-off laughter." The joke is on him, and he sees it all too well:

maddened with despair, so that he laughed loud and long, did Goodman Brown grasp his staff and set forth again ... sometimes the wind tolled like a distant church bell, and sometimes gave a broad roar around the traveller, as if all Nature were laughing him to scorn. ... "Ha! ha! ha!" roared Goodman Brown when the wind laughed at him. "Let us hear which will laugh loudest. Think not to frighten me with your deviltry. Come witch, come wizard, come Indian powwow, come devil himself, and here comes Goodman Brown...." On he flew among the black pines, brandishing his staff with frenzied gestures, now giving vent to an inspiration of horrid blasphemy, and now shouting forth much laughter as set all the echoes of the forest laughing like demons around him.

This is the last laugh Brown ever has, and "his dying hour was gloom." Some modern critics of the story have held that he should have gone on laughing. The effect is, indeed, an almost cosmic catharsis; Brown is laughing at the whole scheme of things, which includes himself. It would be possible to take this as "the moment of truth," but as was said above, he sees the joke too well, and is overmastered by it. His laughter is shock, not acceptance.

Laughter is central to the nightmarish and (literally) lunatic "My Kinsman, Major Molineux." The "shrewd youth" Robin wanders in quest of his kinsman through the moonlit streets of Boston, and horribly finds him. All night the boy has been pursued by inexplicable laughter: the innkeeper's voice, "like the dropping of small stones into a kettle," the "drowsy laughter" of the watchman, "the pleasant titter" of a pretty but

equivocal girl. At the end he discovers what he alone in Boston
does not know, that his kinsman Major Molineux is to be publi-
cly shamed by the Boston mob this very night. Robin has to
witness "the foul disgrace of a head grown gray in honor. They
stared at each other in silence, and Robin's knees shook, and his
hair bristled, with a mixture of pity and terror." Yet "a perception of tremendous ridicule in the whole scene, affected him
with a sort of mental inebriety." One by one those who have
earlier laughed at him laugh once more, and a solemn old
citizen, who has earlier scolded the boy for offending his dignity,
now precipitates a universal laugh by himself breaking down.

And lastly, there sailed over the heads of the multitude a great, broad
laugh, broken in the midst by two sepulchral hems; thus, "Haw, haw,
haw,—hem, hem, haw, haw, haw!" . . . Then Robin seemed to hear the
voices of the barbers, of the guests of the inn, and of all who had made
sport of him that night. The contagion was spreading among the
multitude, when all at once, it seized upon Robin, and he sent forth
a shout of laughter that echoed through the street,—every man shook
his sides, every man emptied his lungs, but Robin's shout was the
loudest there. The cloud-spirits peeped from their silvery islands, as the
congregated mirth went roaring up the sky! The Man in the Moon
heard the far bellow. "Oho," quoth he, "the old earth is frolicsome
to-night!"
  When there was momentary calm in that tempestuous sea of sound,
the leader gave the sign, the procession resumed its march. On they
went, like fiends that throng in mockery around some dead potentate,
mighty no more, but majestic still in his agony. On they went, in
counterfeited pomp, in senseless uproar, in frenzied merriment, trampling all on an old man's heart. On swept the tumult, and left a silent
street behind.

This is indeed "weird mockery." The story is raised to greatness by one startling sympathetic touch, "trampling all on an
old man's heart." Yet this is set off by the strange, aerial, fanciful
lyricism of the cloud-spirits in their silvery islands, and the man
in the moon from some children's tale, who finds this dreadful
laughter "frolicsome." Oddly, it is, too. Somehow what com-

menced as hateful ridicule has become pure fun, a joke so big that it is transmuted to a cosmic irony, so soaring that it is beyond passion. For a moment it is wholly cleansed, not triumphant as irony usually is, with the ironist the knowing one in a world of fools. Robin himself is cleansed, by pity and terror, then by healing laughter, directed at poor Major Molineux, but above all at himself. He knows and accepts himself. And this effect is only possible through Hawthorne's weird and delicate playfulness, remote and disengaged.[8]

12

The Themes of Melville's Later Poetry

In his long poem *Clarel* Melville consistently reverts to the sea for metaphor and illustration. The small lattices of Clarel's inn look down on the pool of Hezekiah

As a three-decker's stern-lights peer
Down on the oily wake below . . . ;   (1. 7)[1]

the Illinois prairie of Nathan's boyhood is like the ocean in

Long rollings of the vast serene—
The prairie in her swimming swell
Of undulation.   (1. 70)

An unfriendly rabbi, discouraging Clarel from Ruth's acquaintance, "sat a torpedo-fish with mind / Intent to paralyze" (1. 96), a figure which was used more notably in *Billy Budd* many years later to describe the villain Claggart's hypnotic eyes.

137

Wall-tombs in a cliff-side are

Pierced square along the gloomy steep
In beetling broadside, and with show
Of port-holes in black battleship.

(1. 112)

A depressed group of poverty-stricken Jews resemble penguins "drawn up on Patagonian beach" (1. 134), as Melville, who took a dark view of penguins, had described them on the great Rock Rodondo in his *Encantadas* sketches of the 1850s. Lurking robber Arabs are like sharks, symbols of evil to which Melville's imagination continually recurs. Only the spears of the marauders are visible behind a ridge.

Like dorsal fins of sharks they show
When upright these divide the wave
And peer above, while down in grave
Of waters, slide the body lean
And charnel mouth.

(1. 206)

These are a few examples out of many: the desert is like the ocean, science is a lightship among shoals, the thought of Ruth to Clarel on the pilgrimage is like a ship fading in the distance.

Significantly, too, Melville resorts to the sea for the background of his "devotees," perhaps his favorite characters, men who have been tried and almost broken, who have learned to accept the burden of life with patience, humility, and—in some fortunate cases—faith. Rolfe, the writer's self-portrait, looks wistfully back to his adventurous youth, even as "a truant ship-boy overworn" (2. 140). The saint Nehemiah's past is clouded, but one version of it makes him an overconfident ship captain broken in to the truth by a series of disasters. The fullest association with the sea, however, comes through the elderly timoneer, a mild ancient mariner whom the pilgrims encounter at the monastery of Mar Saba. He has connections in his past experience with the story of Jonah, and in the same tale ("The Timoneer's Story," 2. 58f.) with the reversed-compasses theme which Melville had touched upon in *Moby Dick* and was to take up twice more in *The Haglets* and *The Admiral of the White*. Except in *Moby Dick* the erring compasses lead directly to shipwreck on a lee shore. The timoneer's adventures are always chastening and usually ominous. He preludes the strange loss of Mortmain's skullcap with his tale of "Man and Bird," (2. 129f.), and in his account of "The Island" he draws a specific parallel between Palestine and the hellish Galapagos of *Encantadas*.

The great tortoise of the Encantadas is a symbol of helpless subjection to chance, time, and fate. Melville associates him with the patient timoneer himself, and with the long-suffering donkey of Palestine and the Levant, but because of his size, his reptilian strangeness, and his incredible longevity the tortoise is most impressive of the three, and most horrible. He is an almost-eternal sufferer.

A hideous, harmless look, with trace
Of hopelessness; the eyes are dull
As in the bog the dead black pool:
Penal his aspect; all is dragged,
As he for more than years had lagged—
A convict doomed to bide the place;
A soul transformed—for earned disgrace
Degraded, and from higher race.

(2. 171)

Like the tortoise, though without the suggestion of "earned disgrace," the timoneer is a victim of life. He has

Nature's own look, which might recall
Dumb patience of mere animal,
Which better may abide life's fate
Than comprehend.

(1. 172)

The donkey is the most amiable sufferer of the three, who represent Melville's sympathy with the underdog and more broadly his sorrowful conception of man. In his 1856–1857 *Journal of a Visit to Europe and the Levant* he had recorded his sympathy with this humble beast of burden: "Donkey is one of the best fellows in the world. It is the patience & honesty of the donkey that makes him so abused & despised. He is so useful & indispensable, that he is contemned. He is so unresisting. Tipe of honesty, &c." In *Clarel* the donkey is represented by the pearl-gray ass, "wonted to man and used to fate" (1. 167), that is ridden by the saintly Nehemiah. He survives his rides, and appears significantly on several occasions.

John Marr and other Sailors (1888) portrays another of Melville's devotees as title-character, and like *Clarel* it links the sea and the land. John Marr is an old sailor, in peaceful but lonely exile in the ocean-like prairies of the Illinois of the 1830s. Like other Melville victims of fate, he is caught by life and inescapably fixed; his wife and family, for whom he left the sea, are dead, and the farmers among whom he dwells can give him little sympathy or understanding. The poems of *John Marr* are songs of exile from another place and time, expressions of irremediable melancholy and loss. At the same time, there is a serenity in them not present in *Clarel* and other earlier works, a subtle and complex state of mind containing both peace and a sort of *horror vacui* imaged in the prairie itself, "the bed of a dried-up sea" where "blank stillness would for hours reign unbroken." One would not stress the serenity too far above the bleak emptiness that goes with it. Very probably the tone of the *John Marr* poems accurately represents the dominant strain of the aging Melville, at once calmer and more hopeless than the doubt and sporadic violence of *Clarel*.

John Marr and other Sailors, a small collection of sea pieces, is more consistent and aesthetically more satisfactory than *Battle-Pieces* or *Clarel*, perhaps because it is less ambitious and briefer. In it a more relaxed Melville turns to his past, now remote and idealized by long assimilative reflection. The themes of *John Marr* are traceable to earlier fiction and poetry of his, and some of them occur still later in *Billy Budd*. John Marr, the exiled sailor, resembles the earlier Israel Potter, who suffered a long Babylonian captivity. We have already noted the prairie-and-sea relationship, which goes back to *Clarel* and still further to *Moby Dick*. Marr wistfully recalls the childlike prelapsarian seamen of a vanished age,

Barbarians of man's simpler nature,
Unworldly servers of the world,

and these are to be found in all the earlier sea-novels—though not so clearly outlined—as well as the later *Billy Budd*. In natural proximity are celebrations of the heroes and the beautiful, poetic vessels of sail, before the naval Iron Age, such as can be found in *Battle-Pieces* and in *Billy Budd*. A pervasive nostalgia for the past is inseparable from these, as is the death theme characteristic of Melville, and an historical and commemorative purpose most evident in *Battle-Pieces* among his earlier works. The indifference of nature in the cruel and capricious sea is an element in more than one poem; there are the devotees of fate, resembling Nehemiah and the timoneer of *Clarel*; and there is the heavy and ominous tread of doom, as in *The Scout toward Aldie* (*Battle-Pieces*) and of course most prominently in *Moby Dick*. *Bridegroom Dick*, the longest of the John Marr poems, goes back directly to *White-Jacket*, with a significant change, however, in point of view.

John Marr, a poem with an explanatory prose introduction of some length, contains an analysis of an aspect of American history as well as a study of one of Melville's unfortunates or devotees. The Illinois prairie of 1838, upon which Marr is cast away, is peculiarly lonely, and thus it represents Melville's ocean. But it is lonely because it is an interim, a moment of America. The Indians whose natural property it is have been exterminated or exiled, along with the bison. The march of civilization, on the other hand, has not yet overtaken it. Only the prairie hen and occasional migrations of pigeons give it life;

scattered settlements and oak groves form widely separated islands in its empty wastes. For John Marr the past is represented by the graves of his wife and children, mingled with a broader and remoter association in Indian mounds. The mode of travel and communication is the prairie schooner, and the traveller steers as if at sea, by the sun. Among undulations like long green swells the white canvas of the wagon peeps out from rank vegetation like a far-off sail at sea. Thus a moment of history merges with Melville's sensibility and experience. Typically, also, there is no remedy for Marr's plight, his loneliness. He has known from his seafaring past "geniality, the flower of life springing from some sense of joy in it," but will know it no more among Illinois farmers alien to his earlier life. Thus the emptiness which is allied to the serenity of the *John Marr* volume.

John Marr is an affirmative poem, since Marr asserts the reality of the heart's memories. Yet the total effect is piercingly melancholy because of the suggestions of illusion that continually arise. Marr's shipmates are "like phantoms of the dead." They are, indeed, "lit by that aureola circling over any object of the affections in the past for reunion with which an imaginative heart passionately yearns" but the yearning is stronger than the comforting realization.

Since as in night's deck-watch ye show,
Why, lads, so silent here to me,
Your watchmate of times long ago?

The sailors of "time long ago" were courageous, childlike fatalists who bore up bravely under a hard life. Most significantly, perhaps, they were endowed with the power to bear. *John Marr* is reminiscent of Coleridge's wistful *Dejection*:

There was a time when, though my path was rough,
This joy within me dallied with distress
And all misfortunes were but as the stuff
Whence Fancy made me dreams of happiness:

For hope grew round me, like the twining vine,
And fruits, and foliage, not my own, seemed mine.

So John Marr's shipmates, not "holding unto life too dearly,"
were

Skimmers, who on oceans four
Petrels were, and larks ashore.

These are unfallen men, who for their youth at least have es-
caped the primal curse by lack of involvement in it.

    John Marr, like the following *Bridegroom Dick*, is literally an
"ubi sunt" poem, and like *Bridegroom Dick*, though less elaborately, it uses the primitive catalogue method of Homer, or the
Old English elegiast, or Dunbar's *Lament for the Makaris.*

Whither, whither, merchant-sailors,
Whitherward now in roaring gales?
Competing still, ye huntsman-whalers,
In leviathan's wake what boat prevails?
And man-of-war men, whereaway?

The death theme, the corpse that disappears in fathomless
depths, is as usual present, and signalized here by one brilliant
line:

Do yet your gangway lanterns, streaming,
Vainly strive to pierce below,
When, tilted from the slant plank gleaming,
A brother you see to darkness go?

The final stanza, however, recalls from death by affirming a
resurrection, a permanent union of the heart, a confidence that
what has been must always be. Melville skillfully follows his
design of images by linking the heartbeat to an earlier line, "If
now no dinned drum beat to quarters," and by making the
memory a muster of seamen:

143

A beat, a heart-beat muster all,
One heart-beat at heart-core
It musters. But to clasp, retain;
To see you at the halyards main—
To hear your chorus once again!

The conclusion, shifting from "musters," is once again a cry, anguished or merely wistful. The muster has been accomplished, but clasping, retaining, is another thing. The poem ends on a possibly cruel illusion.

Bridegroom Dick, the longest piece in the *John Marr* collection, is a storehouse of Melville themes and motifs. It is drawn chiefly from the cruise of the frigate *United States* in 1843–1844 that led to *White-Jacket* (1850). Dick, the old sailor, now reminiscing in dramatic monologue to his old wife, was in his distant youth the "bridegroom" of fortune; popular for his cheerfulness, he was coxswain of the Commodore's gig, and then

… though but a tot for such a tall grade
A high quartermaster at last I was made.

Dick was like the young sailor that John Marr remembers, and his persona makes *Bridegroom Dick* a far mellower production than *White-Jacket*, recounting affectionately circumstances that had filled a younger Melville with democratic indignation. He is happily humble to the *Laced Caps*, the officers, where White-Jacket was heartsickened at the contrast between their natural selves and their "quarterdeck faces." For Dick it is proper that

… a limit there was—a check, d'ye see:
Those fine young aristocrats knew their degree.

Hollow Captain Claret becomes strong Captain Turret, and officers and men alike good and human.

The picture is idealized, but not sentimentalized. Dick has a sharp eye for the anomaly of the military chaplain, "preach-

ing 'tween the guns—each cutlass in its place—" and the ship's
surgeon standing by at a flogging,

Though functionally here on humanity's side...
Never venturing a caveat whatever may betide.

In the long roll are those who have gone down before fate
and fortune, Dainty Dave and Lieutenant Chock-a-Block.

Where sails he now, that trim sailing-master,
Slender, yes, as the ship's sky-s'l pole?
Dimly I mind me of some sad disaster—
Dainty Dave was dropped from the navy-roll!
And ah, for old Lieutenant Chock-a-Block—
Fast, wife, chock-fast to death's black dock!
Buffeted about the obstreperous ocean,
Fleeted his life, if lagged his promotion.

Unlike Melville, Dick has fought through the Civil War, and
he echoes *Battle-Pieces* (*On the Slain Collegians*, *Lee in the Capitol*,
and *A Meditation*) and Ungar in *Clarel*, on the tragic dilemma
of the southern soldier or sailor, faced with a choice too
difficult for the most skillful casuist.

We sailors o' the North, wife, how could we lag?—
Strike with your kin, and you stick to the flag!
But to sailors o' the South that easy way was barred.
To some, dame, believe (and I speak o'what I know),
Wormwood the trial and the Uzzite's black shard.

To Dick, as in the *Battle-Pieces*, the war is from fate and the
gods, and not of human agency. Here he permits himself a
mordant, Lear-like irony:

But, lord, old dame, so spins the whizzing world,
A humming-top, ay, for the little boy-gods

Flogging it well with their smart little rods,
Tittering at time and the coil uncurled.

At this his wife shrinks, to be equivocally reassured,

But sour if I get, giving truth her due,
Honey-sweet forever, wife, will Dick be to *you!*

This vision of the wanton boy-gods is the *truth.*

Dick, like Ungar, despises the comfortable Mammonites who profited from the war. Reechoing *Battle-Pieces*, he celebrates the wooden *Cumberland*, which sank "stilettoed by the *Merrimac's* tusk," and memorably laments the grand old navies of sail— "Their long shadows dwarf us, their flags are as flame." He concludes on a familiar note of warning,

Take in your flying-kites, for there comes a lubber's day
When gallant things will go, and the three-deckers first.

This suggests the words of an old conservative Mexican rancher in *Clarel*, who is accustomed to exclaim, "Stand by, stand by for the great stampede!" and it is reechoed in the *John Marr* volume in *Old Counsel:*

Come out of the Golden Gate,
Go round the Horn with streamers,
Carry royals early and late;
    But, brother, be not over-elate—
All hands save ship! has startled dreamers.

The death theme runs through John Marr, in the elegiac ubi sunt poems just touched upon, in *Tom Deadlight, The Haglets, The Aeolian Harp, Far Off-Shore, The Berg,* and *Pebbles.* The ominous march of doom is most evident in *The Haglets,* where three seabirds steadfastly pursue the fated flagship of the white. The "shadowing three"

... follow, follow fast in wake,
Untiring wing and lidless eye—
Abreast their course intent they take;
Or sigh or sing, they hold for good
The unvarying flight and fixed inveterate mood.

At the end, with the wrecked ship in the breakers, the haglets
enact a dance of fate—they spin in and out like shuttles in the
rigging, they cross and recross, they weave and inweave,

Then lock the web with clinching cry
Over the seas on seas that clasp
The weltering wreck where gurgling ends the gasp.

Melville ends *The Haglets* with a remarkable and ghastly contrast. The admiral and his men lie forever in sleep, enchanted
in the depths of the wizard sea, and about them, in stately lyric
measures,

On nights when meteors play
And light the breakers dance,
The Oreads from the caves
With silvery elves advance;
And up from ocean stream,
And down from heaven far,
The rays that blend in dream
The abysm and the star.

After the terrible struggle of the admiral and his men this exquisite silver calm of nature, idealized in Oreads and silvery elves,
is more shuddery than assuring. The final lines leave the sleep-
ers forever inscrutably in the center of things, the blended
abysm and star.

The ominous haglets are also inscrutable representatives of
an unknowable fate and reality—"the sea-fowl here, whose
hearts none know." *Moby Dick* is of course Melville's most impressive symbol of the ultimate blankness, the faceless whale

whose horror is enhanced by his whiteness. In the *John Marr* volume the man-of-war hawk and the ghastly white Gorgonian shark (*The Maldive Shark*) continue the theme, most explicit in the concluding *Pebbles*, a loosely related group of fine stanzas semi-independent of each other. The first asserts the independence of the sea-winds:

Pintado and gannet they wist
That the winds blow whither they list
In tempest or flaw.

In the second the voice of the conch shell is ultimate, unchanging truth, inspired by the sea. In the third the waters are indifferent:

. . . echoes the seas have none;
Nor aught that gives man back man's strain—
The hope of his heart, the dream in his brain.

The fourth and fifth remark man's precarious position; he "sails on sufferance" on "the old implacable Sea." The sixth asks the Blakeian lamb-and-tiger question of power and goodness so obsessively present in Melville's mind, the painful mixture of reality represented in *Clarel* by mild Christ and terrible Jehovah:

Curled in the comb of yon billow Andean,
Is it the Dragon's heaven-challenging crest?
Elemental mad ramping of ravening waters—
Yet Christ on the Mount, and the dove in her nest!

The last stanza is the finest, and rather startling, since it firmly voices an acceptance, through a paradoxical figure.

Healed of my hurt, I laud the inhuman sea—
Yea, bless the Angels Four that there convene;

For healed I am even by their pitiless breath
Distilled in wholesome dew named rosmarine.

The Angels Four are the four winds, the rosmarine is sea dew. One does not know quite how much weight these lines can bear. They may be a mere momentary flash of wit, playing on the literal benefits of rosmarine. The term has, however, rich symbolic potential, and the opening line is memorable.

Timoleon (1891), like *John Marr and Other Sailors*, was printed in a tiny edition of twenty-five copies. Its poetry, for the most part the product of Melville's old age, is of even higher quality. As its title indicates, it has much to say of ancient Greece, its spirit, its art, and its law. From the romantic organicism voiced in *Moby Dick* Melville now turns explicitly to admiration for classic restraint and finish, which he emulates in his verse. The change is not complete or absolute, and it is not sudden; but change it is, and poems on art, *The Weaver, In a Garret, Art, The Attic Landscape, The Parthenon, Greek Masonry*, and *Greek Architecture* strike the note:

Not magnitude, not lavishness,
But Form—the Site:
Not innovating wilfulness,
But reverence for the Archetype.

(*Greek Architecture*)

It need not be felt that Melville in appreciating has wholly adopted the Grecian ideal; his poems are objective, dramatic, and tentative. Yet the emphasis is ineluctably significant.

On the evidence of *Timoleon*, Melville was seeking a synthesis rather than an exclusion in his altered theory of art. He appears to be tightening and supplementing organicism rather than banishing it. His most notable utterance, in fact, employs the organicist terminology, but with unusual concentration upon the struggle of artistic creation.

In placid hours well-pleased we dream
Of many a brave unbodied scheme,
But form to lend, pulsed life create,
What unlike things must meet and mate:
A flame to melt—a wind to freeze;
Sad patience—joyous energies;
Humility—yet pride and scorn;
Instinct and study; love and hate;
Audacity—reverence. These must mate,
And fuse with Jacob's mystic heart,
To wrestle with the angel—Art.

(Art)

What is said here sounds very much like Coleridge's romantic criticism, as it could be found, for example, in the *Biographia Literaria*. The reconciliation of opposites, the organic vitalist terms of life, pulsing, melting, fusing, and the heart, are all highly Coleridgean. Effort and struggle are more forcefully realized in Melville; one reason for this would be that in discussing artistic creation Coleridge generally had Shakespeare in mind as his ideal, whereas Melville is thinking of his own problems, in more specifically workmanlike terms. His romanticism has come to be, however, the complex and carefully balanced Coleridgean doctrine and not the more daring and radical organicism typical of America, as it is represented in Emerson and Whitman. His "reverence for the Archetype" is possible to square with the organicist metaphor of growth, but it takes some doing; even, be it said, although the idea of the archetype can be found in the arch-organicist Blake.

The problem of goodness and power, which was noticed in *Pebbles* of the *John Marr* poems, is more thoroughly examined in *Timoleon* and in *Fragments of a Lost Gnostic Poem*.

Needs goodness lack the evil grit
That stares down censorship and ban,
And dumfounds saintlier ones with this—
God's will avouched in each successful man?

Timoleon and Timophanes are brothers of ancient Corinth. Their mother prefers the tyrant Timophanes to the good and scrupulous Timoleon, who has saved his brother's life in battle; this represents the frequent verdict of the world. Timophanes becomes Corinth's despotic ruler, but Timoleon, after long for-bearance, at last reluctantly rids the city of its tyrant in a decisive act of illegal justice. He is widely condemned and ban-ishes himself voluntarily to colonial Sicily. At length distin-guished service wins him approval and vindication in his native city:

And Corinth clapt: Absolved, and more!
Justice in long arrears is thine:
Not slayer of thy brother, no,
But savior of the state, Jove's soldier, man divine.

Corinth invites Timoleon back in triumph, but he refuses, and remains in peace and honor in Sicily. In his long exile he has appealed to the gods for some sign of approval, some guarantee that meaning and justice exist. Melville leaves it an open ques-tion whether Timoleon's vindication is the witness.

Or, put it, where dread stress inspires
A virtue beyond man's standard rate,
Seems virtue there a strain forbid—
Transcendence such as shares transgression's fate?
If so, and wan eclipse ensue,
Yet glory await emergence won,
Is that high Providence, or Chance?
And proved it which with thee, Timoleon?

High providence, or chance? Melville remains silent, and Timoleon's refusal of Corinth is also the refusal of an answer. The *Lost Gnostic Poem*, however, gives one, so exactly apposite and opposite to Blake, whom Melville had read, that it is proba-bly a direct answer to Blake's glorification of spiritual energy and daring:

Indolence is heaven's ally here,
And energy the child of hell:
The Good Man pouring from his pitcher clear,
But brims the poisoned well.

This is not necessarily intended as a definitive statement, but it represents Melville's distrust of affirmations.

An enigmatic group of poems, *The Night-March*, *The Ravaged Villa*, *The Margrave's Birthnight*, *Magian Wine*, and *The Garden of Metrodorus*, deals with the central problem of faith, the invisible God, which for Melville is tragic and glorious, but comic too and in some aspects sinister. In *The Night-March* the chief is so far out ahead of his legions that he is lost in distance,

Afar, in twinkling distance lost,
(So legends tell) he lonely wends
And back through all that shining host
His mandate sends.

So legends tell. *The Margrave's Birthnight* develops the theme most fully. The people are summoned every year to the Margrave's castle to keep their lord's birth-night; but, strangely, he never appears.

May his people feast contented
While at head of board
Empty throne and vacant cover
Speak the absent lord?

So accustomed, however, are the guests to his absence that they do not marvel at it, "mindless as to what importeth." To the toilworn peasants it is enough that they feast, and thus in their plenty Melville glances obliquely at the sacrament of communion:

Ah, enough for toil and travail,
If but for a night
Into wine is turned the water,
Black bread into white.

The Margrave's Birthnight evokes, perhaps ironically, the marvel of faith itself, the altar, the religious observance, the rich dwelling, for a thing unseen. The conclusion is ambiguous—pity, admiration, and contempt for mindless indifference are all to be found in it. The poem is less an ironic commentary upon real faith than upon the inadequacy of the worshippers, in whom custom has dulled their perception of the significance of their ritual.

One poem, *After the Pleasure Party*, treats of the tragic dilemma of sex. It has been given much attention, and has been variously interpreted. Some critics have taken it as a direct reference to Melville's own problems. Howard Vincent points out, however, that the speaker is a woman, and that the poem is a dramatic monologue with a definite situation. The woman, a highminded scholar who has scorned sex, suddenly finds herself desperately, ludicrously, jealously in love with a young man. " 'Tis Vesta struck with Sappho's smart," and the smart is unendurable. There is no solution to her tragic dilemma. The young man cannot love her, nor can she cease loving; nor, so far as that goes, would she be assuaged if her love were requited, for she has not ceased to despise sexual passion. She is thus trapped in dualism and contradiction, and paraphrases Plato's myth of the sexes and man's permanent incompleteness.

Could I remake me! or set free
This sexless bound in sex, then plunge
Deeper than Sappho, in a lunge
Piercing Pan's paramount mystery!
For, Nature, in no shallow surge
Against thee either sex may urge,
Why hast thou made us but in halves—
Co-relatives? This makes us slaves.
If these co-relatives never meet

Self-hood itself seems incomplete.
And such the dicing of blind fate
Few matching halves here meet and mate.
What Cosmic jest or Anarch blunder
The human integral clove asunder
And shied the fractions through life's gate?

The problem is universal, and one need say of Melville only that
he is deeply concerned with it as a tragic duality, without feeling
that any strong or peculiar personal application should be
brought home to him. "Cosmic jest" and "anarch blunder" are
always possibilities in his world. Clarel found himself vacillating
between the human love of Ruth and the possibilities of a love
purely divine, as represented by a celibate at the Mar Saba
monastery, and was suddenly smitten with a sense of the tragic
mystery of sex. It should be remarked that *After the Pleasure Party*
presents a thoroughly pagan view of the question—which may
be partly a dramatic limitation.

The *Timoleon* volume, after all, is undoubtedly intended to
present the classic Greek attitude as Melville saw it, with the
partly didactic purpose of appraising Christianity and his own
nineteenth-century culture in its light. Several poems strongly
set forth a timeless, changeless ideal, which Melville admired
from his study of ancient Greek thought and civilization. Two
of these, *Lone Founts* and *The Enthusiast*, steadfastly assert the
truth and cleaving to it despite all discouragement. *Lone Founts*
gives the pattern:

Though fast youth's glorious fable flies,
View not the world with worldling's eyes;
Nor turn with weather of the time.
Foreclose the coming of surprise:
Stand where Posterity shall stand;
And, dipping in lone founts thy hand,
Drink of the never-varying lore:
Wise once, and wise thence evermore.

154

This is a powerful statement for unvarying truth, which can be known from enlightened study of the past. *The Enthusiast* also advocates adherence to the light and the truth through every confusion and danger:

Nor cringe if come the night:
Walk through the cloud to meet the pall,
Though light forsake thee, never fall
From fealty to light.

In candor, however, one must heed the lurking irony of the poem's title, reinforced by a motto, "Though He Slay Me Yet Will I Trust In Him." Certainly Melville admires the enthusiast's courage, but he has left grounds for doubt of his wisdom.

The Bench of Boors and *Lamia's Song* are reactions against the high thinking of *Lone Founts* and *The Enthusiast*. The poet, wakeful in bed, muses on a Dutch genre painting by Teniers of drinkers in an inn, at once envying and despising their drowsy content in their warm, dark inn room. The contrast is explicit in all three stanzas. In the first, "A wakeful brain / Elaborates pain," while the "beery losels" "laze and yawn and doze again." In the second stanza "thought's ampler bound / But chill is found," but

Within low doors the basking boors
Snugly hug the ember-mound.

In the third, "thought's eager sight / Aches overbright." The eyes of the boors are closed, and they take catnaps "in pipe-bowl light." It may be overreading to find a definite point in *Lamia's Song*, but its adjuration,

Descend, descend!
Pleasant the downward way—

suggests a parallel to *The Bench of Boors*, a dramatic reaction to high and lonely speculation on truth. *Lamia's Song* recalls the contrast of the Poet and the brooding Empedocles in Arnold's *Empedocles on Etna*.

Akin to the poems of the Greek ideal are those which, in comparing ancient to modern civilization, celebrate order and law. More than once throughout his work Melville expresses his admiration for the great *Pax Romana*, and he identifies "the Age of the Antonines" particularly as the zenith of the Roman Empire. It was "a halcyon Age"; a period free from demagogues; a time when thought and faith were one. With no hope of immortality, men faced the facts:

The sting was not dreamed to be taken from death,
No Paradise pledged or sought,
But they reasoned of fate at the flowing feast,
Nor stifled the fluent thought.
We sham, we shuffle while faith declines—
They were frank in the Age of the Antonines.

The Romans kept order and degree, and there were few parvenus. Their law was honest, and their emperor was a god, elected by heaven as the foremost and best of men. The poem concludes with the wish that America's future might contain an "age restored of the Antonines." *The Apparition* compares Constantine's vision of the cross of Christ in air with the sight of the Parthenon "first Challenging the View on the Approach of Athens." The pagan symbol has its virtues and advantages. It does not promise supernatural redemption, but it is the best that man can offer.

With other power appealing down,
Trophy of Adam's best!
If cynic minds you scarce convert,
You try them, shake them, or molest.

Against these poems of classic paganism stand two supernaturalists, Hebrew-Egyptian evocations of the godhead, drawn from Melville's Near East tour, like *Clarel*. In *In the Desert* the noon sun is the almost unbearable being of God.

Holy, holy, holy Light!
Immaterial incandescence,
Of God the effluence of the essence,
Shekinah intolerably bright!

The Great Pyramid, of which Melville has spoken impressively in his journal, is an awesome image of God. In the journal he had written that "it was in these pyramids that was conceived the idea of Jehovah. Terrible mixture of the cunning and awful." Moses, he thought, had carried the lore of the Egyptians to the Hebrews. He notes that on the pyramids the stones are utterly bare, "*no vestige of moss upon them. Not the least. Other ruins ivied. Dry as tinder. No speck of green.*" He was to make this same observation about the stones of Palestine. In either instance they are seared by the spiritual force of deity. So, in the poem,

Shall lichen in your crevice fit?
Nay, sterile all and granite-knit:
Weather nor weather-strain ye rue,
But aridly you cleave the blue
As lording it.

The pyramids perfectly present the enormous image of a transcendent God. "They must needs have been terrible inventors, those Egyptians [*sic*] wise men. And one seems to see that as out of the crude forms of the natural earth they could evoke by art the transcendent [novelty] of the pyramid so out of the rude elements of the insignificant thoughts that are in all men, they could by an analogous art rear the transcendent conception of a God." The poem puts it thus:

Craftsmen, in dateless quarries dim,
Stones formless into form did trim,
Usurped on Nature's self with Art,
And bade this dumb I AM to start,
Imposing him.

The journal adds, "But for no holy purpose was the pyramid founded." It has previously said that the creator of the pyramid "was that supernatural creature, the priest." Melville's feelings are complex, and his conclusions subtly balanced. In the prose passage the priest seems an object of horror, and he has created God—yet the priest himself is "that supernatural *creature*" [italics mine], and the God he has created is a true God. There is truth, it appears, in classic, Hebrew, and Christian beliefs alike, though in the *Timoleon* volume the more limited and (with reference to Melville's own day) more honest classic paganism is favored. "We sham, we shuffle while faith declines."

Other Melville themes appear more briefly in *Timoleon*. "Pausilippo," that hill of Naples so lovely that it is reputed to be able to comfort sorrow, is examined and its claims rejected: "It unravels not the pain." Nature, as in *John Marr* and earlier, has no cure for man, as Benito Cereno had found in the story of the 1850s. "See," says his friend Delano, "yon bright sun has forgotten it all, and the blue sea, and the blue sky; these have turned over new leaves." But Cereno is not comforted. "'Because they have no memory,' he dejectedly replied; 'because they are not human.'" And in *Off Cape Colonna* of *Timoleon* the columned cape serenely saw

The wolf-waves board the deck,
And headlong hull of Falconer,
And many a deadlier wreck.

Eden, or the Golden Age, appears in two poems of Greece, *The Archipelago* and *Syra*. The islands of the archipelago are a stricken Eden that Melville compares to the still-flowering Eden of the Marquesas—"'tis Polynesia reft of palms." (One might remark here that Thor Heyerdahl speaks of visiting the valley of Taipi and finding it empty and deserted.) On Syra the dress and demeanor of the inhabitants

Blab of grandfather Saturn's prime
When trade was not, nor toil, nor stress,
But life was leisure, merriment, peace,
And lucre none and love was righteousness.

Melville generally treats the modern Greeks he has encountered as Saturnians, the Polynesians of the North. His merry young hedonists who come from time to time to relieve the austerities of *Clarel* are for the most part Greek Islesmen.

The body of poems unpublished in Melville's lifetime lacks the coherence of his published volumes, for the most part, and these poems date from various, sometimes undetermined periods of his life from about 1859. The greater number of them presumably come from his old age. Two long poems, *In the Hostelry* and *Naples in the Time of Bomba*, companion pieces under the title of the *Marquis de Grandvin*, were probably written, however, between 1857 and 1859. They are drawn from Melville's visit to Naples, recorded in the *Journal of a Visit to Europe and the Levant*. A group of poems called *Weeds and Wildings with a Rose or Two* seems to be a mixture of relatively early and late with the late predominating.

With this uncertainty about dates it is impossible to trace any definite development of theme in Melville's unpublished poems, but for the most part they fall into thematic groups. A number celebrate the downtrodden weed, useless and in danger in a utilitarian world; the hedonist theme of the rose, on the other hand, is also prominent; among the more casual and relaxed pieces there are bird poems and two Christmas poems. The problem of the Christian belief in immortal life arises significantly, as well as its countertheme the golden age. Melville's preoccupation with ironic complexity appears in flower-and-skull images, usually in relatively early verse. Perhaps the largest group among these unpublished pieces attack the utilitarian spirit of the age from various points of view, nostalgic, idealistic, hedonist, charitable.

Melville expresses his customary sympathy with the lowly and downtrodden in a series of poems about weeds and other useless growths: *When Forth the Shepherd Leads the Flock*, *A Wayside Weed*, *Inscription*, *The Avatar*, *The American Aloe*, and *A Ground Vine*. In this iron age many a pleasant, humble plant is doomed.

But alack and alas
For things of wilding feature!
Since hearsed was Pan,
Ill befalls each profitless creature—
Profitless to man!

(When Forth the Shepherd)

The old Saturnian bond with nature is broken. Melville writes most pointedly on this theme in *Inscription:*

A weed grew here.—Exempt from use,
Weeds turn no wheel, nor run;
Radiance pure or redolence
Some have, but this had none.
And yet heaven gave it leave to live
And idle it in the sun.

In *The Avatar* the humble sweetbriar is justified and glorified, for the rose-god once took form in it:

Bloom or repute for graft or seed
In flowers the flower-gods never heed.

The rose poems express simple satisfaction in the flowing beauty and life of their flower. They have the role of the hedonists in *Clarel*, who furnish relaxation from the rigors of high thought and belief. They are not remarkable, but their number impresses; and they are important in representing an aspect of Melville, or at the least of it an aspect of reality that he thought should be considered.

Several pieces take up the theme of immortality: *The Rose Farmer*, *Immolated*, *Pontoosuce*, and the prose-and-verse medley *Rammon*. The weight of their evidence indicates rejection both of the belief in and the desire for eternal life. One reports this, remembering that long before (1856) Melville had "pretty much made up his mind to be annihilated," yet taking them only for part of his mind. The rose farmer, who has inherited an estate which is "nigh Damascus," and laved by the rivers Abana and Pharpar, is faced with the problem,

Shall I make me heaps of posies,
Or some crystal drops of Attar?
To smell or sell or for a boon.
Quick you cull a rose and easy;
But Attar is not got so soon,
Demanding more than gesture breezy.
Yet this same Attar, I suppose,
Long time will last, outlive indeed
The rightful sceptre of the rose
And coronations of the weed.

Shall one live, then, for this world or the next; the rose or the attar? The farmer is advised by a "prosperous Persian," whose counsel he seems to accept,

Who, verily, seemed in life rewarded
For sapient prudence not amiss,
Nor transcendental essence hoarded
In hope of quintessential bliss:
No, never with painstaking throes
Essays to crystallize the rose.

Another poem, *The Vial of Attar*, finds no solace in "the Attar poignant" for "the bloom that's passed away."

Immolated is on the face of it an address to the works, "Children of my happier prime," that the poet has destroyed, and as such it is impressive.

Have I not saved you from the drear
Theft and ignoring which need be
The triumph of the insincere
Unanimous Mediocrity?
Rest therefore, free from all despite,
Snugged in the arms of comfortable night.

In the context of Melville's other poems, however, the last two lines take on added meaning, and "immolated" sounds not unlike "annihilated."

Pontoosuce reflects upon the cycle of nature, birth, growth, maturity, decay, and death:

Wane and wax, wax and wane:
Over and over and over amain
End, ever end, and begin again.

"Who sighs," asks the Spring, "that all dies?" She vanishes "leaving fragrant breath / And warmth and chill of wedded life and death." *Rammon*, a prose-sketch with an appended verse-dialogue, turns away from Buddha's "Ever-and-a-Day" to a frankly fabulous eternity of the "Enviable Isles," the old Saturnian dream.

The Golden Age is an attractive alternative to the Christian (or Buddhist) heaven, as in *Clarel*. Rolfe's wistful reminiscence of his South Sea Island was plainly Melville's own nostalgia for Typee, his tropical Eden, and the lure of a sensuous, innocent, carefree, unmercenary Land of Youth remained with him, unlike the W. B. Yeats of *Sailing to Byzantium*, with his embracement of old age. The earlier writer's "visible truth" does not permit of Yeats's reconciliation. Thus speaks Melville in his latter years:

Old Age in his sailing
At youth will be railing
It scorns youth's regaling
Pooh-pooh it does, silly dream;
But me, the fool save
From waxing so grave
As, reduced to skimmed milk, to slander the cream.

The Golden Age preserved the primal bond, the original unity of man and his world, before the Fall and its consequent or casual pride, selfishness, and greed.

In the jovial age of old
Named from gold
Gold was none for Danae's shower;
While forever silvery fell
Down in dell
Bridal blossoms from love's bower.

Melville is in constant reaction against the materialism of his own Gilded Age, in which he finds

Gold in the mountain
And gold in the glen,
And greed in the heart,
Heaven having no part,
And unsatisfied men.

So La Mancha's knight

Rusts and musts
While each grocer green
Thriveth apace with the fulsome face
Of a fool serene.

Among the unpublished poems, in fact, one concludes that the dominant strain is protest against the spirit of the age, utilitarian, selfish, faithless, and materialistic. Melville's heroes are the weeds, the Don Quixotes, the old shipmasters, the faithful re-memberers of a more picturesque, a more believing, a more idealistic past.

13

Melville's *Clarel*
Doubt and Belief

In 1876 Herman Melville published *Clarel*, a massive poem that takes up over 600 pages in the Standard Constable edition. Publication was made possible only by the unsolicited generosity of Melville's uncle, Peter Gansevoort, who paid almost the entire costs. *Clarel* was a delayed product (it is subtitled *A Poem and Pilgrimage in the Holy Land*) of an 1856–1857 tour of Europe and the Near East, undertaken after his last real effort in *The Confidence-Man* at earning money by his pen, to relieve ill health and depression from overwork. Like Melville's early sea-voyaging, his tour was enterprising but not extraordinary for an American, and as a tourist Melville was unusual chiefly by intensification of rather than divergence from American qualities. As traveller he was energetic, intelligent, serious—and by necessity economical. In energy and desire to learn, though not in the scale of his living, he reminds one of Byron on his wanderings.

His venture to the Holy Land was undoubtedly a conscious voyage from the last new territory of the western world to the sources of the spiritual life of the West, in the light of his aware-

165

ness that the American experiment was in some degree a radical break with the past and with Christianity itself, insofar as it implied a substitution of man for God by affirming man's natural goodness and his power to determine unaided his own destiny. In preparing himself to write *Clarel* Melville supplemented the experience of his tour with much study and pondering. In the interval between *Battle-Pieces* and his poem on the Holy Land he remained primarily a writer and a student, though he had no hope of an audience. He was a thoughtful and active reader of significant contemporary literature—chiefly poetry, serious essays, and weighty maxims such as La Bruyère's. On the evidence of his book purchasing between 1860 and 1870, he read in Marvell, Shelley, Schiller, Heine, Béranger (who, oddly, has some influence on his poetry), Thomson, Tennyson, Tom Hood, Moore, Mrs. Browning, Emerson's essays and his *Conduct of Life*, Arnold's poems and essays, his favorite Camoens, William Cullen Bryant, Jeremy Taylor, Hawthorne's tales, novels, and notebooks, Crabb Robinson, Sir Joshua Reynolds' *Discourses*, Shakespeare's sonnets, and Calderon. For *Clarel* his knowledge of Tennyson's *In Memoriam* and Arnold's *Empedocles on Etna*, as witnessed by his underlinings and annotations, is of special importance because of the themes of these poems; while his continued purchases of Shelley and Hawthorne indicate his steady interest in them. The most direct source for *Clarel*, however, is Melville's own record of his 1856–1857 travels, most recently published as the *Journal of a Visit to Europe and the Levant*.

Clarel is a major treatment of the late-nineteenth-century battle of faith and reason, more especially as it became the war between religion and science. Today the most natural form for Melville's material would be a novel of ideas, following Norman Douglas's *South Wind*, Aldous Huxley's novels, and the innumerable imitations of these. In breadth of purpose Byron's *Don Juan* is remotely comparable to *Clarel*, and Melville may have had it in mind. Even now verse is not necessarily inappropriate to the theme, although the specialization of twentieth-century poetry has given few recent precedents. The verse form is capable of lending a richness of feeling, aesthetic distance, and universality that no novel can provide.

The theme of *Clarel* is religious doubt; or in more dramatic terms it concerns the impact of the Holy Land upon men of the West. Clarel, a young American divinity student, arrives in Jerusalem in a state of mind nicely poised between skepticism and belief. He wanders about the city, and after some time becomes affianced to Ruth, the daughter of Nathan, an Illinois farmer who has turned to the Jewish faith and to Zionism through his love of and marriage with Agar. An extremist, as converts often are, he insists against Agar's will on emigrating to Palestine, where at the beginning of the story he is farming while his wife and daughter take shelter in the city, since the lot of a Hebrew farmer among Arabs is hard and dangerous. And in fact Nathan is murdered by marauding Arabs. Agar and Ruth are sequestered for a period by the strict death rites of their people, and Clarel, perforce separated from them, occupies the interval, although with some qualms, in an expedition to the Dead Sea, the Greek monastery Mar Saba, and Bethlehem.

This expedition is a kind of Canterbury pilgrimage in which Clarel joins a number of other tourists, shepherded by an armed escort of Arabs. The company includes representative types, chiefly American with one English parson, Derwent, who plays an important part. The body of the poem consists largely of the discussions that arise from the deeply significant scenes and objects through which the company passes, discussions that expound before the listening Clarel wide-ranging ideas of religion and society, varied shades of doubt and belief, or Christian faith and materialist rationalism. He returns to Jerusalem educated but shaken by the experience of intimate contact with subtle, passionate, and in some cases tragic minds, to seek comfort in the human love of Ruth; only, as he has occasionally foreboded, to find both her and her mother dead of disease. He is cruelly confronted with their funeral outside the walls of Jerusalem at the moment of return. Shattered as he is, the end of the poem has him gradually collecting himself.

Clarel is a major poem of great interest and many virtues, but one must specify at the outset that it fails structurally of attaining unity and development. Clarel's love of Ruth does not combine harmoniously with the pilgrimage framework, the interest of which should arise solely from the interrelations of the pilgrims themselves. The obtrusion of a fundamental human relationship and tragedy into a drama which is after all a conflict of ideas, not men, betrays to us that the dramatis personae are merely chance-met tourists who will part without affecting each other. The stronger reality reveals the thinness of the pretext by which Melville introduces his ideas. And this reflection—that the characters do not genuinely interact with each other—raises the further complaint that the characters do not grow during the poem, since there is no vital medium to foster growth. The battle of ideas is vigorous, but it is not realized in action; it has no apparent consequences.

This defect in the poem is allied to a characteristic quality of Melville, his sense of doom, which sometimes exceeds what appears to be reasonable under the circumstances set before us. The situation and the characters of *Clarel* are presented to us as under a pall from the outset, too heavy to allow of real change or development. This is a mingled fault and virtue, for the effect is at once impressive and monotonous.

It may be best, as both convenient and candid, to discuss and clear away the principal flaws of *Clarel* at once. Melville is at some disadvantage from the nature of his theme, and from the quality of his material. Doubt is a negative, which inevitably hampers his imagination by short-circuiting possible meanings and relationships. He recorded in his journal in 1857 his disappointment with St. John's island of Patmos, which he attributed to "the great curse of modern travel—skepticism. Could no more realize that St. John had ever had revelations here, than when off Juan Fernandez, could believe in Robinson Crusoe according to De Foe." He goes on to account for this effect, or lack of it, largely from the barrenness of the island, as he is again and again to speak of the aridity and the desolation of Judea; but there is perhaps more to the problem than this physical neutrality of his object. He is having to deal as well with over-

whelmingly strong associations, which it is almost his Christian
duty to revere, in objects and places whose significance at the
same time has been dulled by the resort of tourists, which have
become showplaces and thus have been robbed of life and individuality. Most of them have been described in guidebooks.
Finally, most interesting problem of all, the Protestant mind is
unwilling to identify the Christian story with an actual place
now existing: Clarel is immediately dismayed at the physical
Jerusalem, the seat of the miracle.

> What means this naturalistic knell
> In lieu of Siloh's oracle
> Which here should murmur? Snatched from grace
> And waylaid in the holy place!
>
> (1. 3)

Melville's power as a symbolist, a writer who could combine
meaning with the life and solidity of physical things, is well-
known, and it is far from absent in *Clarel*, but it is operating at
a handicap.

Clarel, an earnest young man of good will, seeks to substan-
tiate his faith by knowledge and experience, to assuage his
heart's longing for peace and certainty. But to look for these in
Jerusalem is, he finds, a dangerous venture. Melville had commented in his 1857 journal that "no country will more quickly
dissipate romantic expectations than Palestine—particularly
Jerusalem. To some the disappointment is heart sickening."
Clarel is profoundly depressed by the walled and battlemented
mountain town, closed, blind, inhospitable, touched everywhere
by the past and death. It is a place of lepers, secret foulness,
tombs and funeral processions; even of hell itself in Gehenna
and the black vale of Jehosephat. He is dismayed by the confusion of the creeds, Moslem, Christian, and Jew, the confusion
and bigotry he sees within the Christian faith itself, and the
intermingling of market and temple evident in even such a
shrine as the Church of the Holy Sepulchre. Jerusalem is "that
waste from joy debarred," a city of tombs, "void citadels of

death." He is driven to ask,

> Of the reign
> Of Christ did no memento live
> Save soil and ruin?

(1. 39)

Above all, however, he is anguished by complexity, contradiction, Manichaean irony in all he sees, with the dreadful
possibility that evil is the dominant force. Every witness of
comfort and faith is quickly modified. The rising sun gleams
upon Olivet, but "how indifferent thy beam." Those who
had "hailed the ray" are immediately distracted by the
muezzin's call to Moslem prayer. Clarel and his spiritual
kinsman the Italian Celio, arrested by the infidel cry are led
to reflect ironically that

> The God alleged, here in abode
> Ignored with such impunity,
> Scarce true is writ a jealous God.

(1. 62)

Before the Arch of Ecce Homo Celio, himself presenting the
painful contradiction of a soaring mind in a misshapen body,
is led to think of Christ as a subtle tormentor, forever tempt-
ing to disappoint us, until the "Anguished Face" of the Man
of Sorrows becomes a paralyzing Medusa-like vision of mingled beauty and terror. For Celio

> The head rejects; so much the more
> The heart embraces—what? the love?
> If true what priests avouch of Thee,
> The shark Thou mad'st, yet claim'st the dove.

(1. 53)

And Clarel shares this conflict of heart and head as he

170

encounters his fellow pilgrims to the Dead Sea and Bethlehem.

His earliest friend among these is Nehemiah, a simple man of faith and a saint on earth. Nehemiah believes that the Second Coming and the New Jerusalem are imminent. Scripture is his all-sufficient authority. He sees no evil and no cureless wrongs. As a trusting and tireless evangelizer for his faith his characteristic habit of passing out tracts involves him continually in ironic encounters with strangers. An armed Arab horseman, for instance, picks up the pamphlet offered him by matter-of-factly impaling the word of the Prince of Peace with a spear. On another occasion Nehemiah has to be restrained from forcing his gift upon a robber sheik to whom the printed word is a dangerous spell. Melville makes capital of the fact of Arab reverence for madmen, of which Nehemiah gets the benefit, for it remains an open question whether the evangelist is an inspired visionary or a monomaniac. The parallel of Pip, the black cabin boy of *Moby Dick*, rises to mind; Pip's madness was the wisdom of the gods.

Only Derwent the Anglican priest and the two Americans Rolfe and Vine are with Clarel on the entire pilgrimage. Derwent (perhaps there is some association with Derwent Coleridge) is a broad churchman, a liberal optimist and believer in progress. So tolerant is he, so willing a compromiser, that he is in danger of compromising the central dogmas of his church. His clothing nicely hits off his combination of clerical and secular:

A cloth cape, light in air afloat,
And easy set of cleric coat,
Seemed emblems of that facile wit,
Which suits the age—a happy fit.

(1. 172)

Derwent habitually sees the bright side of things—quite literally, for he is always first to remark upon a rainbow or a sudden shaft of sunlight. His penchant for ignoring the disagreeable is a frequent source of ironic comment, and he is capable of arousing the more pessimistic of the pilgrims to near-frenzy. Withal he is a good man, and *Clarel* does not condemn his advice to avoid extremes and keep to the pleasant surfaces of life.

Derwent's friend Rolfe is the priest's logical opposite. Rolfe, an American, is experienced, learned, and voluble. To some degree a self-portrait of Melville, Rolfe is inconveniently earnest and lawlessly apt in metaphysical, religious, or social speculation, regardless what dangers may lie at the end of the roads he follows. Clarel is sometimes as discountenanced by Rolfe's inopportune delving as he is by Derwent's superficiality. Rolfe, like Melville, is an ex-sailor who has seen strange lands, and has a particular fondness for the Eden-like isles of the South Seas, which he is at times tempted to substitute for more Christian paradises. He is himself a little exotic and strange, with a touch of wildness in him. In the procession,

> With equal pace
> Came Rolfe in saddle pommeled high,
> Yet e'en behind that peaked redoubt
> Sat Indian-like, in pliant way,
> As if he were an Osage scout,
> Or Gaucho of the Paraguay.

(1. 177)

Vine is suggested by Nathaniel Hawthorne as Rolfe is by Melville. The portrait is gloomily impressive, and recalls Julian Hawthorne's surprised amusement at Melville's conception of his father. Melville persisted, said Julian, in seeing the older Hawthorne as a man burdened with a dark secret, never unbosomed—a notion completely strange to the son, and far more applicable to Melville himself, he felt. Vine is reserved, ambiguous, and imperturbable, but Clarel discerns upon him the effect of some happening so disastrous as to permanently arrest and isolate him. More than any other character Vine has a theme or motif; he is always presented in ambiguous or contradictory terms of light and shadow, austerity and sensuality,

172

sympathy and withdrawal. Singularly pure and unstained by the world, at the same time he is deeply involved in some mystery of blackness, but refined far beyond any vulgar sin. He is "A funeral man, yet richly fair" (1. 111); in his dark background he gleams "as in sombre glade / Of Virgil's wood the Sibyl's Golden Bough" (1. 116). Vine recalls to us Hawthorne's own use of chiaroscuro, such as John Lothrop Motley praised in *The Marble Faun*, and his "freakish mockery, elfin light" (1. 120), which makes one think of Hawthorne's nickname of Oberon and of his narrator, Miles Coverdale, of *The Blithedale Romance*. Clarel is continually attracted to Vine, and makes more than one attempt to achieve his intimate friendship, but he is always delicately rebuffed. (How this parallels the relation of Hawthorne and Melville we are not entitled to say, though we know that the younger man was the more emotional and outgoing). At length a sudden accident, a poignant reference to the face of the dying Savior, causes Vine for once to lose his self-possession. What his own face shows makes Clarel resign further hope of friendship and union; there is something too dark here to be brought into light at all. In the name Vine Melville plays upon "Hawthorne," but his invention leads also to associations with wine and the grape, connoting the rich potentialities concealed beneath Vine's austere surface. At one point Derwent describes him as a black but juicy grape ambushed in leaves (2. 69).

Two other pilgrims, Mortmain and Ungar, are of first importance also. They are both *isolatoes*, the world's castaways; they are in essence such close relatives that Melville does not permit them within the same picture for reasons of emphasis. Ungar appears only after Mortmain has died at the monastery of Mar Saba. Mortmain, a Swede, has been alienated from the very beginnings—to anticipate, he was literally poisoned at the source, for his mother used poison against his life. The illicit child of noble parents, he was reared with "liberal lore / And timely income," but without family ties. He had only "the vague bond of human kind" (1. 187). Thus enfranchised, the young Mortmain resorted to liberal Paris, and buried himself in broad schemes for human betterment; became, indeed, an influential theorist with a following of disciples. Gradually, however, he grew disillusioned with human nature, and correspondingly with political action, finding in the course of events no progress but only a perpetual ebb and flow, an incessant cyclical movement on a shuttle. At the height of his influence, visited by a terrible revulsion, he fled to obscurity, "Oblivion's volunteer to be" (1. 190), and now roams the world a modern wandering Jew, haunted by repentance and something deeper still, "some unrenderable thing . . . deep as nature's mine" (1. 191).

Mortmain, like other characters in *Clarel*, has a distinguishing mark, in his case a black skullcap. This ominous headgear is his protest and also his protection, like the slouch hat that Ahab pulls low over his eyes; and as with Ahab it is at last carried off by a bird of the air, a symbolic emissary of affronted higher powers. Yet Mortmain's sin has been only his faith in human nature.

Mortmain is a victim and a symptom of the Old World's evil; Ungar, who succeeds him, is the living witness of the latter fall, the appearance of evil in the New World of America. For he is a southerner, a Confederate veteran who has fled his country after the Civil War and now lives as a wandering mercenary soldier. Ungar is the embodiment of the old ills and oppressions latent even in the western Eden. He is the descendant of the English Catholics who took refuge in Maryland, and also of American Indians. Himself an opponent of slavery, in the crisis of decision he has followed the loyalties of his region. Irremediably embittered by defeat and its consequences, aggravated as they were by what he regards as the hypocrisy of the victors, he is a savage and trenchant critic of American capitalist democracy. Both he and Mortmain, it should be observed, are firm believers in supernaturalism, though neither has the comfort of a definite creed. In this respect they are reliable representatives of Melville himself.

Clarel is a dramatic poem, in which opinions are relative to the characters who utter them; and as a poem about doubt it is appropriately and consistently doubtful. It does not push to definite conclusions. Yet the creative impulse behind it was undoubtedly Melville's desire to express himself on the issues which most occupied his mind, and the main outlines of his beliefs are sufficiently distinct in *Clarel*, as distinct as a creative artist (as opposed to a philosopher) can or should make generalizations. Since the poem contains an epilogue, which may reasonably be taken for Melville's own summary of his argument, we may at this point turn directly to it, remembering that it follows after an interval the death of Clarel's betrothed, Ruth, and catches Clarel in the process of adjusting himself to his tragic loss.

If Luther's day expand to Darwin's year
Shall that exclude the hope—foreclose the fear?

Unmoved by all the claims our times avow,
The ancient Sphinx still keeps the porch of shade
And comes Despair, whom not her calm can cow,
And coldly on that adamantine brow
Scrawls undeterred his bitter pasquinade.
But Faith (who from the scrawl indignant turns),
With blood warm oozing from her wounded trust,
Inscribes even on her shards of broken urns
The sign o' the cross—*the spirit above the dust!*

Yea, ape and angel, strife and old debate—
The harps of heaven and dreary gongs of hell;
Science the feud can only aggravate—
No umpire she betwixt the chimes and knell;
The running battle of the star and clod
Shall run forever—if there be no God.

Degrees we know, unknown in days before;
The light is greater, hence the shadow more;
And tantalised and apprehensive Man
Appealing—Wherefore ripen us to pain?
Seems there the spokesman of dumb Nature's train.
But through such strange illusions have they passed
Who in life's pilgrimage have baffled striven—

Even death may prove unreal at the last
And stoics be astounded into heaven.

Then, keep thy heart, though yet but ill-resigned—
Clarel, thy heart, the issues there but mind;
That like the crocus budding through the snow—
That like a swimmer rising from the deep—
That like a burning secret which doth go
Even from the bosom that would hoard and keep;
Emerge thou mayst from the last whelming sea,
And prove that death but routs life into victory.

(2. 297–298)

The opening question is obviously to be answered with "No," as the third stanza indicates with "science the feud can only aggravate." In the body of the poem the sole representative of science, Margoth the geologist, is treated very unfavorably, as himself almost a kind of ape. Margoth is flatly a materialist out to shatter all belief in the reality of the spirit, and his geological hammer is emblem of his creed of destruction. Melville adds a tinge of pity to the portrait, since the pretensions of religion rouse Margoth to sincere rage at what he regards as superstitious fraud, but among the pilgrims he is a minority of one, and is treated with distant contempt as a man of ill will. His most vigorous tirade is interrupted by the braying of an ass—an incident which the laconic Vine neatly underlines in two words.

Margoth represents, of course, not all science but the scientist who usurps territory to which he has no claim. Science indeed casts a light, but the shadow is correspondingly greater. Rolfe finds that the freedom now gained by the mind had not released us from the citadel; we only

May rove in bounds, and study out
The insuperable towers about.

(1. 253)

Alternatively, the light of science reveals to us only the shoals amid which we are imprisoned:

> Much as a lighthouse keeper pines
> Mid shoals immense, where dreary shines
> His lamp, we toss beneath the ray
> Of Science' beacon.

(1. 255)

Man is in the plight deliberately symbolized by Melville's earlier hero, Bartleby. Permitted to range the prison yard, with its portion of sky and green grass, Bartleby turns his face only to the wall of The Tombs. The great realities remain "unmoved by all the claims our times avow."

These realities are represented in the epilogue to *Clarel* by the figure of the ancient Sphinx and the personifications of Despair and Faith. The Sphinx is all that we can know of God through the intellect, and despair and faith are the only deep and important reactions that man may have to Him. The bitter but spiritual-minded Mortmain experiences both. Mortmain demands to be left alone in the desert, within sight of the Quarantania, the Mount of the Temptation of Christ. The desert is the place of truth unveiled, the terrible abode of God, of which Melville had said in his *Journal*, "Is the desolation of the land the result of the fatal embrace of the Deity? Hapless are the favorites of heaven." God's embrace is also his curse, for the aspect of Judea is "a caked depopulated hell . . . visaged in significance / Of settled anger terrible" (1. 217). To this region Mortmain fearlessly subjects himself. He is gone long enough to raise fears for him, but presently he gives notice of himself in an inscription chalked on a rock, his "pasquinade," the burden of which is "Estranged, estranged: can friend prove so?" (1. 302). When he reappears he has been blasted; like John from the desert he cries

> Repent! repent in every land
> Or hell's hot kingdom is at hand!

A modern prophet of doom, he recites, as Rolfe sadly comments, "The dire *Vox Clamans* of our day" (1. 314). Despite efforts to restrain him, he makes the symbolic gesture of drinking Dead Sea water, to the warning,

Sip the Sodom waters dead;
But never from thy heart shall haste
The Marah—yea, the after-taste.

(1. 315)

Thus he has taken upon himself the full burden; he has sipped of the bitter waters, the wormwood and the gall, which are associated with the Dead Sea in the following canto (1. 318).

Here Melville interposes to give an explicit interpretation of Mortmain through the device of a dialogue between two hovering spirits, "sad with inefficacious love." Can so tortured a man, so overmastered by the vision of evil, be himself free from evil? "May a sinless nature win / Those deeps he knows?" The reply is decisive:

Sin shuns that way;
Sin acts the sin, but flees the thought
That sweeps the abyss that sin has wrought.
Innocent be the heart and true—
Howe'er it feed on bitter bread—
That, venturous through the Evil led,
Moves as along the ocean's bed
Amid the dragon's staring crew.

(1. 321)

Mortmain has known the depths of despair, and is to know faith before he dies. At the convent of Mar Saba he is strangely visited by the mercy of heaven. As he perches on a lofty crag a gier-eagle knocks off his skullcap by pecking at it—an odd, but as a bystander remarks not an unprecedented occurrence—and he is left "bareheaded brooding" (2. 125). Mortmain's cap is both his armor and his badge of isolation. The importance of this casual incident is emphasized by a parallel a few pages later in the canto, "Man and Bird" (2. 129–130). The eagle is an agent of God, who has laid Mortmain open to final mercy.

A single palm tree amid the rocks (which Melville had seen and remarked upon in his *Journal*) catches Mortmain's eye. He is so moved by the symbol, like Gabriel's "lily-rod" at the Annunciation, that

He felt as floated up in cheer
Of saint borne heavenward from the bier.

(1. 137)

Transported, he vows to invoke the palm at the moment of his death, which he feels is hard upon him ("Comfort me then, thou Paraclete!"), and the aspect of his body when it is found suggests that the pact has been kept. An eagle feather is lying on the lips of the dead Mortmain.

To return to the words of the epilogue, Melville's thought is unmistakably dualist in *Clarel*, with ape and angel, heaven and hell, star and clod, and light and shadow. In Faith's sign of the cross, the spirit above the dust, is the traditional body-and-soul opposition of Christianity, and the question of man, "Wherefore ripen us to pain?" dismisses any possibility of accepting pantheism, organic monism, or the doctrine of evolutionary growth. Melville dismisses as firmly as T. E. Hulme the notion of change in either God or man. And his treatment of the development of Nathan the converted Zionist reveals how unsatisfactory he found pantheism or the cycle of nature.

Nathan, a thoughtful boy on the lonely Illinois prairie, was converted to deism by encountering the work of Tom Paine (1. 72), and as has often happened deism led to pantheism:

The god, expelled from given form,
Went out into the calm and storm.

(1. 73)

Pantheism was all very well in its aspect of growth and fertility, but with Nathan it could not survive the impact of his mother's death upon him. Growth and development imply also decay and death:

Let now the breasts of Ceres swell—
In shooks, with golden tassels gay,
The Indian corn its trophies ray
About the log-house; is it well
With death's ripe harvest?

This disillusion aided in bringing about his conversion to the Jewish faith. One is reminded of Eliot's *East Coker*, with its harvest festival and final "eating and drinking. Dung and death."

In dualism and contradiction the world must remain forever—Melville is of course more Manichaean than sorts with approved Christian orthodoxy—"if there be no God." Here a distinction must be made between the broad sweep of human history and the life of the individual—also between natural or human and supernatural experience. To Melville all history demonstrates the fall of man by its contradictions and failures. Man's mixed nature means perpetual dualism and strife. We are not entitled to believe in a God in the sense of a deus ex machina, who will intervene to solve our difficulties. It is within God's power to intervene at any moment, but our historical experience seems to show that he is unlikely to do so in the near future. On the other hand, only those human societies which are based on faith can long survive.

Bonds sympathetic bind these three—
Faith, Reverence, and Charity.
If Faith once fail, the faltering mood
Affects—needs must—the sisterhood.

(1. 102)

In this belief Melville is at one with T. S. Eliot in his *Idea of a Christian Society* and *Notes towards the Definition of Culture*.

God, however, is remote from us, and in his remoteness seems cruel, as Emily Dickinson poignantly complains:

I know that he exists
Somewhere in silence;
He has hid his rare life
From our dull eyes.

Therefore for Melville as for uncounted others Christ the God and Man, the divine sufferer, must complete the conception. It might be added that God the Father is too purely male, the stern sky-god; consequently Melville's Christ is relatively feminine and passive, the more as there is no room in his system for the virgin mother of God. In any event his thought is consistently dualist and supernaturalist.

Yet the gap between the natural and the supernatural presents us with a fearful difficulty: we cannot *know* God in this world. To bridge this gap the epilogue resorts to the contrast of illusion or appearance and reality—rather gingerly, it must be confessed.

Even death *may* prove unreal at the last,
And stoics be astounded into heaven.

There is a touch of amused self-irony in the second line, for Melville's own attitude in his later years was decidedly stoic, and one cannot identify him completely with his advice to his young hero Clarel. It is significant that at one point (2. 243), he couples Christ with Marcus Aurelius.

The final appeal is to the heart, with its intimation of immortality. Regarded superficially, this would appear to be the doctrine of Derwent, the optimistic Anglican priest; but undoubtedly Melville's conception of the heart is far deeper and more complex than any he attributes to Derwent. His advice is given to a Clarel who has suffered much and been thoroughly tested, after he has used his intellect to the limits of his capacity. Through the heart he will rise, emerge even "from the last whelming sea." The figures here suggest the Christian paradox of life through death, or true life in place of the false life of mortal appearance. They remind one of Lycidas, who

> sunk low, but mounted high
> Through the dear might of Him that walked the waves.

Perhaps surprisingly, they suggest still more strongly Shelley's *Prometheus Unbound*, in which appearances give way to the eternal truth, and Shelley's last line, "This is alone Life, Joy, Empire, and Victory!" is surely the source of Melville's.

References to America in *Clarel* are highly critical, as Melville takes the privilege of a friend to point out weaknesses and to advise. His observations have much the same import as in his *Battle-Pieces*. The attempt to create a secular Paradise, in which men trust wholly in themselves, is doomed to disaster, as is the effect to separate the future from the past of humanity. Man is not self-sufficient, humanitarian reform is by itself worthless, and a stable society must be based upon spiritual faith in supernatural powers. The lofty-minded Celio rejects America in his search for a better world, in favor of ancient, devoted Palestine.

> They vouch that virgin sphere's assigned
> Seat for man's re-created kind:
> Last hope and proffer, they protest.
> Brave things! sun rising in the west;
> And bearded centuries but gone
> For ushers to the beardless one.
> Nay, nay; your future's too sublime:
> The Past, the Past is half of time,
> The proven half.

(1. 49)

Quite naturally the embittered Ungar is the severest critic of

America, and his arguments are both lengthy and valuable. But one speech alone must suffice here to represent the prevailing point of view in *Clarel:*

> Hypothesise:
> If be a people which began
> Without impediment, or let
> From any ruling which foreran;
> Even striving all things to forget
> But this—the excellence of man
> Left to himself, his natural bent,
> His own devices and intent;
> And if, in satire of the heaven,
> A world, a new world have been given
> For stage whereon to deploy the event;
> If such a people be—well, well,
> One hears the kettledrums of hell!
> Exemplary act awaits its place
> In drama of the human race.
>
> (2. 247)

At this point Rolfe asks Ungar, with decided pertinence, whether such an act is certain. He receives the confident answer that it is; God and man are always the same, and an honest reading of history permits of accurate prediction of the inevitable disaster.

14

Melville's Poetry

Any conclusions about Melville's poetry must be qualified. His poetic achievement is impressive, and today it strikes us as incomparably higher than that of most of his American contemporaries, but his verse is experimental and uneven. Whether for lack of public encouragement or informed criticism or for other reasons, only infrequently do we find a poem of Melville's completely satisfying; few of them have received that last touch that endues with consummate harmony and pervasive life, the perfect fusion of meaning and form. On the other hand, few of Melville's poems are devoid of at least some interesting lines, some sudden flash of imagination or vital glow of thought.

Robert Penn Warren in his well-known essays has stressed the modernity of Melville's poetry: its expressive qualities, its occasionally "metaphysical" metaphor, its daring excursions both in theme and diction beyond the conventionally "poetic," as in the use, for example, of legal or other technical, nonpoetic terminology. It furnishes support for the new critical stand against the presumption that any subject matter, material, or image is valuable as such, independent of its function within the organic unity of the poem. This emphasis upon the forward-looking qualities of Melville's poetry is just, so long as one bears in mind that Melville's experiments are frequently romantic or Victorian, and sometimes are even Elizabethan, or Caroline, or Miltonic.

The variety and elaboration of his stanza forms and metres is remarkable, and this variety is characteristic both of the English romantic poets and the Victorians, from whom Melville undoubtedly received important help. Here a distinction needs to be made which has an important bearing upon Melville's "modernity." The conceptions of genre and of superficial form that a romantic or a Victorian poet included among his assumptions were not those of the twentieth century, in which genre and considerations like stanza pattern have gone far toward dissolution. Whatever freedom the romantic aspired to, he nevertheless had in mind some model to begin with or to depart from. With all his value for spontaneity, irregularity, intensity, and flexibility, he did not aim at sheer expressiveness; he did not abandon his notion of a preconceived framework. His variety, in short, rested upon a prior regularity; he thought of himself as writing a *kind* of poem, a pseudo-Pindaric ode, a ballad, an epistle, a blank verse meditation. So also thought Melville, in whose verses some preexisting and still-undissolved model can almost always be perceived.

Melville tried his hand at many different types and metres, which I will try to describe summarily, without, however, always maintaining strict logical distinction of category, since determinations by metre, stanza form, subject matter, development, point of view, and basic method (narrative, lyric, dramatic) inevitably overlap. He experimented with the pseudo-Pindaric ode (*The Conflict of Convictions*), with the ballad, especially in *Battle-Pieces*, in various metres and stanzas, often with a refrain; with pastoral lyrics and songs, from Shakespeare to Wordsworth in their echoings; with short epitaphs, epigrams, and gnomic stanzas; with dramatic monologues and character sketches; with panoramic narratives of Civil War battles and with didactic narratives like *Timoleon* and *After the Pleasure-Party;* with verse epistles like *To Ned* and *To Daniel Shepherd;* and once with the blank verse Coleridgean "conversation" poem in *On the House-Top.* He is most daringly experimental in his single narrative poem in a dramatic frame, *Donelson,* which purports to be read straight from news bulletins; in two verse medleys or symphonies, *The Marquis de Grandvin* and *The Parthenon,* which remind one a little of W. B. Yeats's *Nineteen-Nineteen* or his *Meditations in Time of Civil War;* and in several prose-verse medleys, *John Marr, Rip Van Winkle,* and the unfinished *Rammon,* all three of which contain a prose introduction as important as and inseparable from the verse that follows. One should mention, too, an apparent use of almost purely accentual lines in most of the poems of *John Marr and Other Sailors,* perhaps owing something to the metre of Coleridge's *Christabel* although very different in effect.

A summary of Melville's poetry leaves a reader with several principal impressions: that, rather surprisingly, Melville almost never uses the standard iambic pentameters of English poetry, his staple, as in *Clarel,* being the four-beat line; that he is seldom fully lyrical and subjective, his emotions and meditations almost always fixing upon general and as it were public objects, situations, and ideas; and that, correspondingly, he is preponderantly an objective and dramatic poet.

Melville almost never uses blank verse, possibly because as a poet he is deliberately submitting himself to metrical discipline and consequently prefers to keep his distance from a measure that approaches the cadence of prose, for which his appetite has been amply satisfied elsewhere. Tetrameter, stricter yet more matter-of-fact and colloquial, suits him better. He is not a master of the melody of tetrameters, like Milton in *L'Allegro* and *Il Penseroso* or Keats in his *Ode to Fancy;* he combines an almost mechanical regularity of beat with a variety attained by harshness of sound and wrenching or flattening of stress. Newton Arvin remarks that "a slow, weighty, tight, and rather toneless line that stubbornly refuses to give the ear an inappropriate pleasure" is characteristic of Melville. One struggles to define this characteristic effect, which is close to the effect of Melville's most successful later prose. Its tone is heavy, sometimes harsh, leaden but somehow empty or at least lacking some expected quality, despite its weight. It is nevertheless impressive as the organic expression of Melville's temperament and sensibility, and is generally dramatically appropriate to his themes. His set lyrics and songs, for example, have a weighty stiffness, a ponderous roll, which is not without its strength:

Noble gods at the board
Where lord unto lord
Light pushes the care-killing wine:
Urbane in their pleasure,
Superb in their leisure—
    Lax ease—
Lax ease after labor divine!

(Ditty of Aristippus)

The "ditty" is a heavy, sonorous roar.

At his poorest, usually in verse that would seem to be relatively early, in some *Battle-Pieces*, in *The Marquis de Grandvin*, and in most of the "rose-poems," Melville can be cloyingly over-fluent, grotesque without expressiveness, and monotonously repetitious both of sound and of word, with a pitch and vehemence quite disproportionate to his meaning. It is an ungrateful task, however, to catalogue faults, and it seems hardly necessary to warn readers against a small proportion of Melville's poetry, which presents no overpowering lure in the first place and which certainly no critics are importuning us to accept. One passes on, therefore, to discussion of better and more typical verse. The peculiar quality of Melville's characteristic line comes at least in part from flattening-out or sometimes wrenching of stress. Thus, in *John Marr*, for example, the accents would presumably fall as I indicate in these two verses:

In levíathan's wáke what bóat preváils?
And mán-of-wár's men, whéreaway?

Yet the unstressed syllables tend to break their bounds and seek equality. Other instances out of many are

Implacable I, the old implacable Sea:
Implacable most when most I smile serene—
Pleased, not appeased by myriad wrecks in me

from *Pebbles;* lines such as "And shied the fragments through life's gate" and "While Amor incensed remembers wrong" from *After the Pleasure-Party;* "Cat-naps take in pipe-bowl light," from *The Bench of Boors;* and from *In a Bye-Canal* the memorable "Twixt the whale's black flukes and the white shark's fin."

As was previously remarked, Melville's variations do not lie within accepted patterns, like slurs and trills in melody, but suggest a more radical departure, a reaction, almost a revolt from a mechanically regular scheme preestablished by himself. His shifts are less elements of harmony than positive changes of tempo or reversals of stress pattern. In stanzas of any complexity he almost invariably seeks to change the direction of the movement or even to reverse it, and few stanzaic poems of any length are without some decided break. In *Misgivings* the speed of the first four lines is clogged by the fifth, which introduces a quite different movement, like a near-halt before a change of direction.

When ocean-clouds over inland hills
Sweep storming in late autumn brown,
And horror the sodden valley fills,
I muse upon my country's ills—
The tempest bursting from the waste of Time
On the world's fairest hope linked with man's foulest crime.

There is a similar break in *The March into Virginia*, which corresponds to a shift in the sense:

Did all the lets and bars appear
To every just or larger end,
Whence should come the trust and cheer?
Youth must its ignorant impulse lend—
Age finds place in the rear.

The final line is ungainly in its sudden pauses and concluding
rush, but it is appropriate and powerful.

Ungainliness is deliberately sought in *A Utilitarian View of the
Monitor's Fight*, and achieved by a comparable short line, along
with intentional deprivation of the rhyme the ear demands:

Plain be the phrase, yet apt the verse,
More ponderous than nimble;
For since grimed War here laid aside
His painted pomp, 'twould ill befit
    Overmuch to ply
The rhyme's barbaric cymbal.

The well-known *Monody* on Nathaniel Hawthorne is an interesting instance of a larger shift, in which despite an identical
pattern of stresses, six lines each of alternating four and three
accents, the movement and tone alter greatly. The first stanza
is meditative, clogged, irregular, wandering; the exquisite second stanza, Melville's grief externalized and calmed in delicate
images, is fluid, melodious, and straightforward in its motion
toward the climactic close (here one needs to remember Vine
in *Clarel* and his characteristic grape motif):

To have known him, to have loved him
After loneness long;
And then to be estranged in life,
And neither in the wrong;
And now for death to set his seal—
Ease me, a little ease, my song!

By wintry hills his hermit mound

The sheeted snow-drifts drape,
And houseless there the snow-bird flits
Beneath the fir-trees' crape:
Glazed now with ice the cloistral vine
That hid the shyest grape.

Melville's departures from regularity, one concludes, are connected with his instinct for dramatic complexity and contrast, and with his desire to explore all the potentialities of the situation he has established in his poem, even if they should lead him to discordance and contradiction.

15

Billy Budd
The Order of the Fall

Interpretation of *Billy Budd* has been copious and elaborate, with the natural result that in some instances at least it has reached the stage of overrefinement. Two views of Melville's novella are interesting heresies, disastrous in their implications but persuasive enough so that they cannot be ignored. One is the notion that the irony which *Billy Budd* unquestionably contains is of a type which directly reverses the overt meaning of the story; the other, closely related, asserts the presence of a hidden interior narrator behind the apparent third-person narrator whom we would generally identify with Melville. According to this reading, the ostensible narrator is shallow, conventional, and platitudinous, while the concealed narrator is keen and malignant, a bitter mocker behind a bland façade. Both of these views are provocative, and both are destructive and false. At the risk of unfairness, however, they will be dismissed without formal refutation in this essay. Tracking down heresies is dangerous and disagreeable. One is likely to get lost in the process, and in notably unpleasant surroundings. I will therefore offer a few observations only.

The irony imputed by some critics to *Billy Budd* would if it existed be cheap, puerile, and perverse. This masterpiece of Melville's old age contains ironies and ambiguities aplenty, but they are such as arise naturally from profound meditation upon a tragic theme of great magnitude. They do not reverse the direct statements upon which our sense of the meaning rests, but modify, enrich, and complete them. Likewise the division of the narrator into two is unwarranted by any evidence, and lessens rather than enhances the interest and aesthetic value of the story. The teller of *Billy Budd* is not Melville in any abstraction of Melville "the man," but Melville in relation to the imaginative stuff he is working, and this Melville-the-man-and-the-artist is quite complex enough to encompass both assertion and negation, the hope and the fear, the generality and its completion by the particular. The "hidden narrator," in fact, is merely a fabrication of the critic to convey his own sense of "Melville the man" as a secret malcontent too cowardly to speak out. Acceptance of him would make an intellectual and artistic chaos of the story.

Rejection of these heresies, however, need not deny the complexity of *Billy Budd*. Melville has no fixed beliefs to guide him through the fundamental and tremendous issues of good and evil, of innocence and experience, indeed of basic reality, that his story engages. One is concerned, not to minimize its difficulties, but to reassert the good faith along with the value of Melville's final pursuit of truth. Much is positive in *Billy Budd:* the sense of tragedy, the celebration of heroism, the commemoration of the past, the archetypal pattern of the Fall of Man, the meaning of political events, and the ultimate acceptance of the principle of divine justice. It is a story not of diminution but of magnification; not of Aristotelian comedy but of Aristotelian tragedy. As in *Moby Dick*, Melville is exigent of the fullest respect for his action:

Passion, and passion in its profoundest, is not a thing demanding a palatial stage whereon to play its part. Down among the beggars and rakers of the garbage, profound passion is enacted. And the circumstances that provoke it, however trivial or mean, are no measure of its power. In the present instance the stage is a scrubbed gun-deck, and one of the external provocations a man-of-war's spilled soup.

This conception of tragedy is of course Wordsworthianly romantic as well as Aristotelian, but the drama of *Billy Budd* is played out against a very spacious and critical background:

The year 1797, the year of this narrative, belongs to a period which as every thinker now feels, involved a crisis for Christendom not exceeded in its undetermined momentousness at the time by any other era of which there is record.

Billy Budd is a tragedy, in that it presents an action of great magnitude which develops a dilemma insoluble without loss of one good in the preservation or achievement of another. Or, in other words, two different and irreconcilable systems, in this instance the order of nature and the order of the British Navy, clash directly. Captain Vere is forced to choose the order of the navy and therefore sacrifice the innocent Billy Budd, the natural man. We sympathize with Vere, but such is the complexity of the considerations involved that we are not quite sure that he has chosen rightly; there are some grounds for arguing that the sacrifice of Billy was avoidable. There is a tragic reconciliation, however, for the memory of Billy lives on as a Christ of the sailors, as a bright spot of meaning and hope against a dark background. His kingdom is not of this world, but it exists. *Billy Budd* is tragedy, too, in providing the increase of knowledge that we have rightly come to attach to tragedy. The confrontation of opposing characters in crucial action, if properly conducted, enlarges our knowledge of the potentialities of human nature and of the circumstances under which human beings exist. Perhaps it should be added, though in any event no exact alignment is being attempted here, that *Billy Budd* differs from classical tragedy in introducing positive and fundamental evil as the immediate cause of the catastrophe in the person of the master-at-arms, Claggart. Without this irrational and inexplicable element of evil, which functions as chance, the order of nature and the order of the navy under the Mutiny Act might have lived together without an open breach.

This essay proposes to emphasize the large affirmative elements of *Billy Budd*, which make of it a celebration rather than a condemnation of reality and its mysterious master. Melville, however, in keeping with his time and his own nature, is dealing with an ultimately unknowable universe which it is nevertheless his paradoxical purpose to know. Given the scope and complexity of the problem and the subtlety and range of the author's mind (to separate them arbitrarily), no easy certainties can be expected. All the issues, in fact, are as difficult as possible. Here a critic might protest that *Billy Budd* is an image, an aesthetic object, and not a metaphysical treatise. One critic at least has persuasively so protested. Yet there are many avenues toward truth, and without rearguing the dispute of literature and belief one can accept the coexistence of a final with a formal cause. Thus assuming the validity of the inquiry, I proceed to the difficulties that complicate the affirmative interpretation of *Billy Budd* that is to be advanced here.

Perhaps the chief of these concerns Captain Vere of the British ship of the line *Indomitable*, aboard which Billy is impressed from the merchantman *The Rights of Man*. Vere is figuratively the God of Billy Budd, although we must be cautious in applying the metaphor, so as to avoid a full and literal identification. Much depends, then, upon the reader's interpretation of him. Is he well-intentioned, beneficent? Is his judgment to be respected? He is certainly used as a symbol for order: nicknamed "Starry" Vere, he represents the steadfast, well-regulated system of the heavens, the ideal of conservatism. Yet it may be asked, "Is this good?" To William Blake it would not have been good; his Urizen, the God of repression and negation, was lord of the stars in their courses, and Melville knew Blake:

Prison'd on wat'ry shore,
Starry Jealousy does keep my den:
Cold and hoar,
Weeping o'er,
I hear the father of the ancient men.

Vere might conceivably be the inexorable agent of the principle of tyranny. Also, if he is well-intentioned, he may be misguided. In carrying out the provisions of the naval code by which he is bound, he apparently violates it in a number of instances. He takes judgment into his own hands; at the fatal court-martial he is arbitrary, so that his officers are seriously disturbed; the procedure at Billy's execution, which is carried out with masterly forethought, is subtly irregular. He could have waited—it would have been more customary to wait—upon the judgment of his admiral, but he hurries Billy to his death.

These are possibilities, for which Melville makes full allowance. Nevertheless the weight of both the internal and the external evidence is strongly against them. As to the evidence in *Billy Budd* itself the question may be asked, is it possible to draw a conclusion at all? Is not Vere a dramatic character in an imagined fictional work, whom the author treats with dramatic objectivity? One answers that no such objectivity is possible to any creator but God himself—the writer aspires to objectivity, he tries to free himself from the limits of his individual mind, but if he succeeded he would be more or less than human, and his work would be more or less than literature. He cannot and should not transcend the limitations of his own vision and emphasis, which are also his identity and his power. Absolute objectivity would be simply confusion and meaningless, dead neutrality. The writer tells us, "Here is the way I see things, here is the evidence. You may if you like interpret my evidence differently." So Melville offers us ample material for divergent interpretations of Captain Vere, but his own is accessible to us in the text of *Billy Budd*. To deny that it can be determined is in my opinion a disastrous conclusion based upon a half-truth.

Captain the Honorable Edward Fairfax Vere is a bachelor

of forty at the time of the action of *Billy Budd*. Melville uses a dialectic method of balanced oppositions to describe him: he is of noble birth, but his advancement has not been altogether owing to his family connections; a stern disciplinarian, he is also mindful of the welfare of his men; he is "intrepid to the verge of temerity, though never injudiciously so"; a thorough seaman and naval officer, he never uses nautical terms in ordinary conversation, and is notably unobtrusive as commander of his ship. In politics he is an enlightened conservative. He represents a golden mean.

He has salient traits and qualities, however, which characterize him more sharply as an unusual man. Though practical enough when occasion demands it, he "would at times betray a certain dreaminess of mood." He is exceptionally bookish, and he reads deeply, in "confirmation of his own more reserved thoughts," and to establish settled principles by study of the past. His fellow officers find him a little pedantic; he cannot quite accommodate his thought and conversation to the "bluff company" of men "whose reading was mainly confined to the journals." Thus he has not quite the tact of a man of the world; he is too honest and direct to pay careful heed to immediate circumstances. His nickname, "Starry" Vere, has come upon him accidentally from a kinsman who had been reading Marvell's *Appleton House*, with the lines

This 'tis to have been from the first
In a domestic heaven nursed
Under the discipline severe
Of Fairfax and the starry Vere.

The connection is casually made, but the association of "discipline severe" with the captain is nevertheless worth pointing out. A lover of order, he is devoted to duty and discipline, and certainly to self-discipline.

Vere is a bachelor, and Melville frequently attaches symbolic importance to the distinction between the bachelor and the married man—to which categories of humanity the monk might also be added. Carefree detachment from the deeper problems of life, however, is generally the hallmark of Melville's bachelors; in particular, they disbelieve in evil and are untouched by it. Captain Delano of *Benito Cereno* and Stubb in *Moby Dick* are bachelors, symbolically though not literally; the Templars of the sketch *The Paradise of Bachelors* are bachelors who have found the perfect freedom from trouble. Captain Vere is not quite like these; his is the disengagement of one set apart for a high and strange destiny. Uninvolved, *Billy Budd* involves him in complex tragedy. This sense of destiny is presumably the reason for his otherwise unexplained "dreaminess of mood." The trait both isolates and exalts him, as one who is to be the priest of dreadful rites and mysteries. Though unconsciously, he looks forward to his great central act.

One notices that Vere resembles Melville himself, in his reading, in his respect for the lessons of the past, especially the history of classical antiquity; perhaps in what ordinary men think of as his pedantry. Melville's well-known disinclination for society in his later years was partly attributable to his hopelessness of being understood. Like Vere no man of the world, he sought some genuine meeting of minds, and was impatient of the usual pleasantries of social intercourse. Most important for our reading of Captain Vere's character, his conservative love of order is shared by the later Melville. This statement is no doubt debatable, but the evidence in support of it is very strong: within *Billy Budd* itself in the introductory sections on the mutinies at Spithead and the Nore, and in the general attitude toward the French Revolution. The Nore Mutineers

ran up with hurras the British colors with the union and cross wiped out; but that cancellation transmuting the flag of founded law and freedom defined, into the enemy's red meteor of unbridled and unbounded revolt. Reasonable discontent growing out of practical grievances in the fleet had been ignited into irrational combustion as by live cinders blown across the Channel from France in flames.

This and comparable passages, I maintain, are to be taken at their face value.

Melville's writing from *Battle-Pieces* onward supports this argument for Captain Vere. The heavily boding introductory poems of the *Battle-Pieces* volume are darkened by the prospect of civil disorder—

When ocean-clouds over inland hills
Sweep storming in late autumn brown,
And horror the sodden valley fills,
And the spire falls crashing in the town,
I muse upon my countries ills.

(*Misgivings*)

The impressive *On the House-Top* is unequivocal in its condemnation of the New York draft rioters:

The Town is taken by its rats—ship-rats
And rats of the wharves. All civil charms
And priestly spells which late held hearts in awe—
Fear-bound, subjected to a better sway
Than sway of self; these like a dream dissolve,
And man rebounds whole aeons back in nature.

True, the suppression of the riots by martial law is partly regrettable, a "grimy slur on the Republic's faith implied," but man's dignity, "never to be scourged," is as "Nature's Roman," living in freedom under law. *Bridegroom Dick* of *John Marr and other Sailors* acquiesces to naval authority as the earlier White-jacket had not, as an inescapable necessity, and one may mention in passing the many signs in the massive *Clarel* of Melville's revulsion from materialist and naturalistic doctrines of unfettered democratic rule and inevitable progress. In the late *Timoleon* volume *Fragments of a Lost Gnostic Poem* reads like a direct attack upon Blake's exaltation of energy unrestrained:

Indolence is heaven's ally here,
And energy the child of hell:
The Good Man pouring from his pitcher clear,
But brims the poisoned well.

and *The Age of the Antonines*, when "Orders and ranks they kept
degree," is set up as an example for Americans to ponder.
Melville praises Greek architecture for

Not magnitude, not lavishness,
But Form—the Site;
Not innovating wilfulness,
But reverence for the Archetype.

Far more could be cited from the poems and prose of the later
Melville to demonstrate their kinship with the convictions of
Captain Vere, but these instances may suffice.

So much for Vere's character. To proceed to his actions,
their wisdom and their honesty are open to question, but this
must always be true of any man's conduct when faced with a
tragic dilemma. We sense that the Captain must play his pre-
destined part in the tragic drama. If he is guilty of a tragic error,
it is in his insistence upon secrecy throughout, or perhaps more
largely in his acceptance of all responsibility for decisions. Yet
here again, the tragic circumstance is unusual, the natures of the
men he deals with exceptional, and chance by accumulation
takes on the purpose and the power of fate.

To rehearse the situation of *Billy Budd*, it is of course abnormal because of the recent mutinies at Spithead and the Nore.
The year 1797 is a time of crisis for the British Navy; there is
no leisure for extended reflection. Then, it happens that Vere
is unusually isolated. Because of a lack of frigates in the English
squadron the *Indomitable*, though a line-of-battle ship, is on detached scouting duty, partly because of her exceptional sailing
qualities and partly because of Vere's reputation for reliability
and initiative. The circumstances conspire to produce tragedy.
Vere is approached by his master-at-arms, with whom it happens by chance that he is not well acquainted, with a tale of

treason in a common sailor, Billy Budd. Behind the charge lies a monstrous tangle of malice and misunderstanding, of which Vere can know nothing. Nevertheless he judges correctly that Claggart's accusation is false. Among the difficulties and ambiguities of the situation is the fact that the skillful and subtle Claggart is strangely clumsy. He overplays his hand; one would say that he is fey, struck by some unconscious premonition of approaching death, or maddened by irrational hatred. This oddity, however, rather confuses than clarifies.

Convinced of Claggart's falseness, Vere arranges a private confrontation, but with the object rather of testing the accuser than of trying the accused. By hindsight we can see that this decision of Vere's is fatal, since the private interview ends with the death of Claggart, struck down by a single blow of the man he has slandered, too unexpected and sudden for prevention. Yet in the circumstances Vere's choice of action would seem eminently judicious. Again Vere contributes to the fatal result indirectly by his very insight and his kindliness, as in his insight into Claggart. He correctly interprets Billy's agonized dumbness before the accusation, but his kindness has precisely the opposite effect from his intentions.

Though at the time Captain Vere was quite ignorant of Billy's liability to vocal impediment, he now immediately divined it, since vividly Billy's aspect recalled to him that of a bright young schoolmate of his whom he had seen struck by much the same startling impotence in the act of eagerly rising in the class to be foremost in response to a testing question put to it by the master. Going close up to the young sailor, and laying a soothing hand on his shoulder, he said: "There is not hurry, my boy. Take your time, take your time." Contrary to the effect intended, these words so fatherly in tone, doubtless touching Billy's heart to the quick, prompted yet more violent efforts at utterance— efforts soon ending for the time in confirming the paralysis, and bringing to the face an expression which was as a crucifixion to behold. The next instant, quick as the flame from a discharged cannon at night, his right arm shot out, and Claggart dropped to the deck.

Vere immediately foresees the full consequences, as his first word indicates. " 'Fated boy,' breathed Captain Vere in tone so low as to be almost a whisper, 'what have you done!' " Henceforth he is to be the agent of the Fates, or perhaps the banishing angel of the latter Fall.

The captain's behavior in the following moments is suspicious, almost mad, to the eye of an observer. The ship's surgeon is immediately summoned. A prudent, poised, and experienced man, he is an excellent witness. His shock, however, comes from his limited understanding of what he witnesses. Vere's conduct is perfectly intelligible by the light of his own superior insight.

Suddenly, catching the Surgeon's arm convulsively, he exclaimed pointing down to the body—"it is the divine judgment of Ananias! Look! . . . " Captain Vere was now again motionless standing absorbed in thought. But again starting, he vehemently exclaimed—"Struck dead by an angel of God. Yet the angel must hang!"

The surgeon is further disturbed by Vere's disposition of the body in a compartment of his cabin, as implying an unaccountable desire for secrecy; and, as we have seen, in this respect Vere is consistently laid open to suspicion. The possibility that he is wrong, or even that he is evil, is steadily before us. Yet a reasonable reading demonstrates that Vere's estimate of the situation, affected as it is by mutiny and war, is correct. A fallen and corrupted world can only be governed by the stern provisions of the Mutiny Act, carried out with the utmost speed and decision. No time can be permitted for doubt or speculation by those who might mutiny; in his secrecy Vere is defending an indispensable order. The surgeon is a calm and experienced man of the world, but Vere is endowed with intuitive knowledge of the human heart and spirit, well-fitted, and alone well-fitted on the battleship *Indomitable*, to comprehend two such extraordinary human beings as Claggart and Billy Budd. Along with them he belongs to a different order of nature from common humanity, and he is of tragedy the ideal spectator as well as the agent.

Melville specifically distinguishes, in his discussion of

Claggart's character, between the man of the world and the wise man.

I am not certain whether to know the world and to know human nature be not two distinct branches of knowledge, which while they may coexist in the same heart, yet either may exist with little or nothing of the other. Nay, in an average man of the world, his constant rubbing with it blunts that fine spiritual insight indispensable to the understanding of the essential in certain exceptional characters, whether evil ones or good.

Such an exceptional character is Captain Vere, as is made utterly clear in the account of his final interview with the condemned Billy. This interview is private—the narrator himself does not venture to intrude upon it, so that its precise nature is left in obscurity. Its general purport, however, is unmistakable.

But there is no telling the sacrament, seldom if in any case revealed to the gadding world wherever under circumstances at all akin to those here attempted to be set forth two of great Nature's nobler order embrace. There is privacy at the time, inviolable to the survivor, and holy oblivion the sequel to each diviner magnanimity, providentially covers all at last.

The solemnly hieratic quality of *Billy Budd* is epitomized in the vocabulary of this passage, with "sacrament," "great Nature," "privacy . . . inviolable," "holy oblivion," "diviner magnanimity," and "providentially." The story is concerned both literally and more largely with a mystery. The reference to "great Nature" might lead us to one further reflection: despite the grounds for suspicion of him which Melville himself carefully implants, we can confidently exculpate Captain Vere from the guilt that inheres in the code he carries out because he so thoroughly understands its limitations, and so clearly distinguishes between its empirical measures and the absolute values of divine justice. Vere is genuinely disinterested because he comprehends the entire truth. He himself dies in battle not long after the execution of Billy, and his last words are the murmured "Billy Budd, Billy Budd," but "that these were not the accents of remorse, would seem clear." His death, while fighting the French battleship *Atheiste*, is a fitting consummation of a solemn observance, and is ironic only in the largest sense of tragic irony, a mode quite devoid of mockery.

Melville properly declines to make a definitive statement, although one would suppose that the import of the passages cited above was definite enough. "Whether Captain Vere, as the Surgeon professionally and primarily surmised, was really the sudden victim of any degree of aberration, one must determine for himself by such light as this narrative may afford." The light afforded is surely sufficient, both as regards Vere's wisdom and his good faith. Yet the situation is enormously complex, even in a sense perverse. "In the jugglery of circumstances preceding and attending the event on board the *Indomitable* and in the light of the martial code whereby it was formally to be judged, innocence and guilt personified in Claggart and Budd—in effect changed places."

This jugglery, of course, affects not merely Claggart and Billy but Captain Vere as well, so that the better may frequently seem to be the worser part. Thus at the court-martial all his officers take a more lenient view than Vere's; they seek some compromise to avoid invoking the penalty of death. They are, however, "well-meaning men not intellectually mature," too weak to confront the logic of tragedy. " 'But surely,' " says the good-natured officer of marines, " 'Budd purposed neither mutiny nor homicide.' " " 'Surely not, my good man,' " Vere replies. " 'And before a court less arbitrary and more merciful than a martial one that plea would largely extenuate. At the last Assizes it shall acquit. But how here? We proceed under the law of the Mutiny Act.' " It is to be remarked, incidentally, as part of the jugglery of circumstances by which Vere is made to act outside the code he would enforce in order to achieve the purposes for which it exists, that the presence of a marine "in a case having to do with a sailor" is an infraction of the general custom of the Navy. It is worth noticing, too, that Melville does not spare Vere at the court-martial the tinge of pedantry he has earlier mentioned as one of his attributes. As has been asserted, however, this slight disharmony of Vere's with ordinary minds should be interpreted, although it could be otherwise interpreted, as a mark of his strength and distinction and not of his weakness. One feels that in this matter Melville comes very close to identifying himself sympathetically with his character.

At the court-martial Vere is at first slow to speak, but his hesitation comes of considering how best to fit his words to the capacities of his hearers. "Similar impatience as to talking is perhaps one reason that deters some minds from addressing any popular assemblies."

When speak he did, something both in the substance of what he said and his manner of saying it, showed the influence of unshared studies modifying and tempering the practical training of an active career. This, along with his phraseology now and then was suggestive of the grounds whereon rested that imputation of a certain pedantry socially alleged against him by certain naval men of wholly practical cast.

Vere thus represents something of Melville's own isolation in his age and society, and symbolized in the circumstances of the writing itself of *Billy Budd*, a work for long unpublished. This isolation does not at all preclude an anxious solicitude for the times, and a desire to set men right. Vere may be said to be preaching the necessity of tragedy to his good-natured and reluctant officers, and so, on the whole, is Melville. In a complacent and optimistic age he asserts the doctrine "now popularly ignored," of the fall of man, and directs attention to the neglected words of Holy Writ, to which he recurs.

And, indeed, if that lexicon which is based on Holy Writ were any longer popular, one might with less difficulty define and denominate certain phenomenal men. As it is, one must turn to some authority not liable to the charge of being tinctured with Biblical element. . . . Dark sayings are these, some will say. But why? Is it because they somewhat savor of Holy Writ in its phrase mysteries of iniquity? If they do, such savor was foreign from my intention for little will it commend these pages to many a reader of today.

The irony is minatory. Vere also uses the phrase, "a mystery of iniquity," in lecturing to his officers.

Neither Melville nor Vere is denying the possibility of progress and the existence of providence. The rejection of materialist optimism does not preclude the hope that all may yet be well. More than once in *Billy Budd* it is said that the French Revolution, once deemed an unmixed evil, has functioned in a design to bring about an ultimate good, in which the sacrifice of Billy has its mysterious place as well. But Melville and Vere maintain that this good can come about only through suffering and tragic action; there are no short cuts, no easy solutions. The original sin has alienated man from nature, and therefore no natural code can fitly govern human society. War is a sin; the mutiny at the Nore is a sin against order; and their consequences are the Articles of War and the Mutiny Act. Yet the alienation is not total, we are not wholly estranged from the natural and the divine; and sacrifice can redeem. At the court-martial Captain Vere's movements symbolize his resistance against an inappropriate yielding to nature, his acceptance of the hard and bitter way. "Turning, he to-and-fro paced the cabin athwart; in the returning ascent to windward, climbing the slant deck in the ship's lee roll; without knowing it symbolizing thus in his action a mind resolute to surmount difficulties even if against primitive instincts strong as the wind and the sea." His argument reemphasizes this separation: " 'Though the ocean, which is inviolate Nature primeval, though this be the element where we move and have our being as sailors, yet as the King's officers lies our duty in a sphere correspondingly natural?' "

In connection with the verdict of the court-martial, a verdict of death directed largely by Vere, the famous American case of the brig-of-war *Somers* is referred to as a parallel, although on the *Somers* the sentence of death was carried out "in a time of peace and within not many days sail of home." This case, in which Melville's cousin Gert Gansevoort, an officer on the *Som-*

ers, figured prominently, is "here cited without comment." Yet the following paragraph constitutes a powerful justification of the decision, or at least the decider, in each instance:

Says a writer whom few know, "Forty years after a battle it is easy for a non-combatant to reason about how it ought to have been fought. It is another thing personally and under fire to direct the fighting while involved in the obscuring smoke of it. Much so with respect to other emergencies involving considerations both practical and moral, and when it is imperative promptly to act. The greater the fog the more it imperils the steamer, and speed is put on though at the hazard of running somebody down. Little ween the snug card-players in the cabin of the responsibilities of the sleepless man on the bridge."

The writer "whom few know" is of course Melville himself.

The quotation suggests, in addition to its obvious sympathy with the man in authority, the terrible directness and nakedness of his responsibility. In executing his constituted law he himself stands outside it. Vere as well as Billy Budd must be the sacrifice, as is indicated by the private interview after the verdict, which associates the two as father and son, Abraham and Isaac (or God the Father and God the Son). Immediately after the interview the senior lieutenant of the *Indomitable* encounters his captain. "The face he beheld, for the moment one expressive of the agony of the strong, was to that officer, though a man of fifty, a startling revelation. That the condemned one suffered less than he who mainly had effected the condemnation was apparently indicated." And Vere's duty is to remain agonizing and to a degree equivocal, in the tragic jugglery of circumstances. "In this proceeding [the burial of Claggart] as in every public one growing out of the tragedy strict adherence to usage was observed," it is said. Yet, as has been hinted earlier, this is in a sense not true. Original sin has set all askew, as man is apart from nature; the order of the Mutiny Act is an order subtly distorted, a little perverse. To maintain it Vere must in some degree violate it. Or, to put the action on another level, Vere is the priest-celebrant of a mysterious ceremonial sacrifice, which he must perform with decorum in despite of imperfect assistants and a confused and turbulent congregation, the crew of the *Indomitable*.

Until the sacrifice is consummated the original sin is in power. Its consequences cannot be evaded. "Their Captain's announcement was listened to by the throng of standing sailors in a dumbness like that of a seated congregation of believers in hell listening to the clergyman's announcement of his Calvinistic text." Extraordinary measures are taken, therefore, to ensure that the ceremony is fitly carried out. Special precautions are taken that none shall communicate with Billy (save the chaplain, whose services as Christian priest are irrelevant at this grim observance and unneeded by the victim himself). Certain parts of the ceremony are imperceptibly altered or hastened as the immediate circumstances dictate; regularity is consistently preserved by slight irregularities. Thus at a threatening murmur of the crew its entity as a congregation is suddenly destroyed by calling the starboard watch. "Shrill as the shriek of the seahawk the whistles of the Boatswain and his Mates pierced that ominous low sound, dissipating it; and yielding to the mechanism of discipline the throng was thinned by one half." The comparison suggests the cruel bird of prey, perhaps the exultant emissary of a fierce sky god, like the hawk that was dragged to destruction with the sinking *Pequod* in *Moby Dick*. This, with its implications, is an aspect of the meaning that cannot be ignored, but at the same time it is only one aspect of a very complex totality. To return to the progress of events, Billy's body is then buried with all expedition, "with a promptitude not perceptibly merging into hurry, though bordering that." But "a second strange human murmur was heard" when sea birds pass close to the ship and hover over the spot where the body has vanished into the sea. Immediately the drum beats to quarters, "at an hour prior to the customary one."

That such variance from usage was authorized by an officer like Captain Vere, a martinet as some deemed him, was evidence of the necessity for unusual action, implied in what he deemed to be temporarily the mood of his men. "With mankind" he would say "forms, measured forms are everything; and that is the import couched in the story of Orpheus with his lyre spellbinding the wild denizens of the woods." And this he once applied to the disruption of forms going on across the Channel and the consequences thereof.

Here again form as it were violates form to secure the ends of form. The actions of the sea birds present a complex situation to us. They represent a natural and in some degree a divine order, as the superstitious sailors intuitively sense; they are akin to the "primitive instincts strong as the wind and the sea" against which we have seen Captain Vere resolutely combatting. The imagery of this passage is strongly reminiscent of Melville's impressive ballad of *The Haglets*, the fatal birds that follow the doomed flagship of the Admiral of the White. These seafowl are notable at once for their apparent purposiveness and their absolute alienation from the purposes of man; they are "The seafowl ... whose hearts none know," the "inscrutable haglets," the "shadowing three" that "follow, follow fast in wake, / Untiring wing and lidless eye." Thus the birds that come to the burial of Billy Budd have a dual significance. They are supernatural, but do they mourn or exult? Are they the emissaries of a god of nature who is outraged and pitiful, or of an authoritarian sky god, like Shelley's Jupiter, who forever oppresses the natural man, the "people" of the *Indomitable* and of the world? For Melville's purposes they are both, though these meanings are contradictory; since the possibilities of the situation itself are ambiguous and contradictory.

Immediately upon the second murmur of the crew the drum beats to quarters. "At this unwonted muster at quarters, all proceeded as at the regular hour." The religious ceremony in which Billy Budd has been sacrificed to the observance of the Mutiny Act concludes formally, in terms specifically liturgical. "The band on the quarter-deck played a sacred air. After which the Chaplain went through with the customary morning service. That done, the drum beat the retreat, and toned by music and religious rites subserving the discipline and purpose of war, the men in their wonted orderly manner dispersed to the places allotted them when not at the guns." There is plainly a sharp irony in this mingling of Christianity and war. Vere is the real priest, the Chaplain only a simulacrum. Yet the tragedy must be played out, the redemption must be bought by the blood of the Lamb, and Vere and Billy must take their allotted parts.

Critics have frequently noted the supernatural aura surrounding of the death of Billy, so that he becomes momentarily a second Christ. At the last signal "it chanced that the vapory fleece hanging low in the East, was shot through with a soft glory as of the fleece of the Lamb of God seen in mystical vision and simultaneously therewith, watched by the wedged mass of upturned faces, Billy ascended; and ascending, took the full rose of the dawn." Some physical aspects of the execution are so unusual as to seem miraculous. And at full day "the fleece of low-hanging vapor had vanished, licked up by the sun that late had so glorified it. And the circumambient air in the clearness of its serenity was like smooth white marble in the polished block not yet removed from the marble-dealer's yard." This latter manifestation is not free from ambiguity, with the vanishing of the fleece and suggestion of a tombstone in "the marble-dealer's yard," but the clearness and serenity remain.

Notes

Notes to Chapter 2

1. London and New York, 1948, p. 160.   2. "Coleridge's Conversation Poems," *Quarterly Review* 244 (1925): 284–298.   3. *The Poems of Samuel Taylor Coleridge*, ed. E. H. Coleridge (London, 1912), p. 257n.   4. *The Romantic Comedy* (New York, 1948), p. 160.   5. *Letters of Samuel Taylor Coleridge*, ed. E. H. Coleridge (Cambridge, Mass., 1895), 1: 197. Hereafter referred to as *Letters*.   6. Ed. John Shawcross (Oxford, 1907), 1: 11.   7. *Letters*, 1: 197.   8. *Biographia Literaria*, 1: 43.   9. *Letters*, 1: 197.

10. Ibid., 1: 243.   11. Ibid., 1: 228–229.   12. See Henry J. W. Milley, "Some Notes on Coleridge's 'Aeolian Harp' " *MP* 36 (1939): 365–368.

Recent notable discussions of the conversation poems include Albert Gérard, "The Discordant Harp: The Structure of Coleridge's Conversation Poems," *English Romantic Poetry* (Berkeley and Los Angeles, 1968); and A. R. Jones, "The Conversational and other Poems," in *S. T. Coleridge*, ed. R. L. Brett (London, 1971).

1. This distinction is so frequently made in Coleridge's criticism that it seems pointless to list instances of its occurrence. 2. In this respect the difference between the illusion of dream and the illusion of art parallels the difference between Coleridge's primary and secondary or poetic imagination, since the secondary imagination coexists with the conscious will. See *Biographia Literaria*, ed. J. Shawcross (Oxford, 1907), 1: 202. 3. *Coleridge's Shakespearean Criticism*, ed. T. M. Raysor (Cambridge, Mass., 1930), 1: 126–131. See also "Classical and Romantic Drama" and "Dramatic Illusion," ibid., 1: 196–198 and 199–207. 4. Cf. Aristotle, *Poetics*, 25. 3–5, tr. S. H. Butcher, *Aristotle's Theory of Poetry and Fine Art*, 4th ed. (New York, 1951): "Within the art of poetry itself there are two kinds of faults,—those which touch its essence, and those which are accidental. If a poet has chosen to imitate something, but has imitated it incorrectly through want of capacity, the error is inherent in the poetry. But if the failure is due to a wrong choice—if he has represented a horse as throwing out both his off legs at once, or introduced technical inaccuracies in medicine, for example, or in any other art—the error is not essential to the poetry. . . . First, as to matters which concern the poet's own art. If he describes the impossible, he is guilty of an error; but the error may be justified, if the end of the art be thereby attained . . . if, that is, the effect of this or any other part of the poem is thus rendered more striking. A case in point is the pursuit of Hector. If, however, the end might have been as well, or better, attained without violating the special rules of the poetic art, the error is not justified: for every kind of error should, if possible, be avoided.

"Again, does the error touch the essentials of the poetic art, or some accident of it? For example,—not to know that a hind has no horns is a less serious matter than to paint it inartistically."

Coleridge's doctrine is Aristotelian, but he differs from Aristotle in accepting *surface* improbability as necessary and desirable in a particular genre, the romantic. This difference could be accounted for by reference to his theory of imagination, and correspondingly to his doctrine of the reconciliation of opposites and its application to artistic imitation as the union of sameness with difference. 5. *Biographia Literaria*, 2: 5. 6. *Coleridge's Shakespearean Criticism*, 1: 129–130. 7. Ibid., 1: 198. 8. *Biographia Literaria*, 1: 202. 9. Ibid., 2: 10.

10. It is of some interest that *rich* with its immediate derivatives (such as *richer, richlier, rich-burning*) occurs over sixty times in Coleridge's poetry. See Sister Eugenia Logan, *A Concordance to the Poetry of Samuel Taylor Coleridge* (Saint-Mary-of-the-Woods, Indiana, 1940). Perhaps half of the instances of its use have real weight. I have noticed twelve

significant occurrences of *rich* in *Collected Letters of Samuel Taylor Coleridge, 1795–1806*, ed. E. L. Griggs (Oxford, 1956). 11. *Biographia Literaria*, 1: 202. 12. *The Letters of John Keats*, ed. M. B. Forman (London, 1947), p. 413. 13. May 31, 1830, *Table Talk*, *The Complete Works of Samuel Taylor Coleridge*, ed. W. G. T. Shedd (New York, 1853), 6: 324. 14. As J. L. Lowes conveys, no doubt inadvertently, in *The Road to Xanadu* (Boston, 1927). 15. The concept of difference in sameness occurs wherever Coleridge discusses the distinction between imitation and copy. 16. *Biographia Literaria*, 1: 174. 17. Ibid., 2: 43. 18. "In philosophy equally as in poetry, it is the highest and most useful prerogative of genius to produce the strongest impressions of novelty, while it rescues admitted truths from the neglect caused by the very circumstance of the universal admission. Extremes meet. Truths, of all others the most awful and interesting, are too often considered as so true, that they lose all the power of truth, and lie bed-ridden in the dormitory of the soul, side by side with the most despised and exploded errors" (*Aids to Reflection*, Shedd, 1: 117). To Coleridge this meeting of extremes is generally baneful—some of the horror of "the Night-mare Life-in-Death" is attributable to the juxtaposition of vigorous life with its contrary death, symbolized in glaring contrasts: "*Her* lips were red, *her* looks were free, / Her locks were yellow as gold: / Her skin was as white as leprosy, / The Night-mare Life-in-Death was she, / Who thicks man's blood with cold." 19. "Endymion," 4. 193–194. Perhaps a closer kinship might be mentioned, however, with Blake's habitual personifications of nature, which outside of *The Ancient Mariner* are rarely to be found in Coleridge.

20. In *Mardi*. 21. *Moby Dick*, ch. 23, "The Lee Shore." 22. *Five Poems, 1470–1870* (London, 1948), p. 71. 23. Cf. *Dejection: An Ode:* "And oh! that even now the gust were swelling, / And the slant night-shower driving loud and fast! / Those sounds which oft have raised me, whilst they awed, / And sent my soul abroad, / Might now perhaps their wonted impulse give, / Might startle this dull pain, and make it move and live!" 24. This statement does not, however, preclude the shadow of causality mentioned above, p. 32, in commenting upon Coleridge's reply to Mrs. Barbauld. The simulacrum of necessity, a confusion of *post hoc* with *propter hoc* such as occurs in dreams, is vital to the effect of inevitability. Thus the rising of the moon *seems* to be the cause of the deaths of the mariner's companions: "Till clomb above the eastern bar / The horned Moon, with one bright star / Within the nether tip. / ...One after one, by the star-dogged Moon, / Too quick for groan or sigh, / Each turned his face with a ghastly pang, / And cursed me with his eye." 25. This movement was presumably Coleridge's ideal action for a full-scale poem. It is clearly suggested in the first part of *Christabel*. He talked more than once of the destruc-

tion of Jerusalem as an epic subject with the implication of the Christian dispensation as the redemption of mankind. See April 28, 1832, *Table Talk*, Shedd, 6: 392–393.   26. See Robert Penn Warren, Introduction to *The Rime of the Ancient Mariner* (New York, 1946). Mr. Warren's treatment of the "one life" theme of organic relationship is both full and brilliant.

Discussion of *The Ancient Mariner* is of course extremely extensive. For further representative work see my bibliography, *Romantic Poets and Prose Writers*, Goldentree Bibliographies (New York, 1967), and James Boulger, ed., *Twentieth Century Views of "The Rime of the Ancient Mariner,"* Spectrum Books (Englewood Cliffs, N. J., 1969).

Notes to Chapter 4

In addition to Lowes's famous *Road to Xanadu* (Boston and New York, 1927), and Elisabeth Schneider's *Coleridge, Opium, and Kubla Khan* (Chicago, 1953), the poem has been treated in at least one more full-scale study, Marshall Suther's skilful and profitable *Visions of Xanadu* (New York, 1965), which synthesizes previous work. John Beer concisely reconsiders its sources in "Poems of the Supernatural," *S. T. Coleridge*, ed. R. L. Brett (London, 1971), pp. 53–70. Miss Schneider's comments on the versification, structure, and classical bases of *Kubla Khan* in her book and an earlier article have been particularly valuable to me. See also her "The 'Dream' of *Kubla Khan*," *PMLA* 60 (1945): 784–801.

Notes to Chapter 5

1. "The Relation of Coleridge's *Ode on Dejection* to Wordsworth's *Ode on Intimations of Immortality*," *PMLA* 50 (1935): 224. 2. "The 'Dream' of *Kubla Khan*," *PMLA* 60 (1945): 799. 3. E. de Sélincourt, "Coleridge's *Dejection: An Ode*," *Essays and Studies by Members of the English Association* 22 (1937): 7-25. Also appears in E. de Sélincourt, *Wordsworthian and Other Studies* (Oxford, 1947). See also T. M. Raysor, "Coleridge and 'Asra,' " *SP* 26 (July 1929): 305–324, for the influence of Sarah Hutchinson upon Coleridge's poetry and life. The *Ode* plays an important though subsidiary role in Professor Raysor's argument. 4. See, e.g., S. F. Gingerich, *Essays in the Romantic Poets* (New York, 1929), pp. 45–49; J. W. Beach, *The Concept of Nature in Nineteenth-Century English Poetry* (New York, 1936), p. 123. Both Gingerich and Beach, however, are inclined to consider the subjectivism of the *Ode* a permanent trait of Coleridge's thought, interpreted by Gingerich as "transcendental-

ism" and by Beach as "antinaturalism." See E. Bernbaum, *Anthology of Romanticism*, 2nd ed. (New York, 1948), pp. 1103–1104, for a brief digest of the view implied in my text; at greater length N. K. Stallknecht, *Strange Seas of Thought* (Durham, N. C., 1945), pp. 159–171; also J. Shawcross, Introd., *Biographia Literaria* (Oxford, 1907), p. xliii.   5. The poem expresses and objectifies the mind and the creative process from which it takes its origin. Thus the famous definition of poetic imagination, although it is concerned with the *poet* and *poetry* rather than the *poem*, implies that the critic will commence with the poem and work backward to the complex activity of mind which is its cause. His analysis and evaluation of the poem will be controlled by his conception of the developing structure and unity of the mind behind it. See *Biographia Literaria*, 2: 12–13.   6. Used here to signify belief in the reality of mind and nature both, in agreement with the views of Shawcross, Stallknecht, and Bernbaum.   7. "The symbolical . . . is always itself a part of that, of the whole of which it is the representative . . . the latter [the allegory] cannot be otherwise than spoken consciously;—whereas in the former [the symbol] it is very possible that the general truth may be working unconsciously in the writer's mind. . . . " (Coleridge, *Miscellaneous Criticism*, ed. T. M. Raysor, Cambridge, Mass., 1936, p. 99).   8. Cf. ll. 53–55, 62, 66, 73–75.   9. Gingerich acutely remarks, "Had he [Coleridge] had a profound conviction, such as Poe's, that sorrow and melancholy are the best themes for poetry, he undoubtedly could have written many marvellous poems in a doleful spirit. But like Wordsworth he held that truly creative art must be inspired by joy, that poetry is the spontaneous overflow of powerful feelings." (*Essays in the Romantic Poets*, p. 48.)

10. "It (Imagination) is essentially *vital*, even as all objects (*as* objects) are essentially fixed and dead." (*Biographia Literaria* 1: 202.) If the term "understanding" be objectionable, we may shift our terms and define Coleridge's state of mind as the result of an attempt to disjoin intellect and feeling.   11. See ll. 92–93. In Coleridge's dialectic the antithesis of whole and part is roughly equivalent to the antitheses of reason and understanding, imagination and fancy, imitation and copy, organic and mechanical, genius and talent.   12. See, e.g., Coleridge's statement specifically in terms of the poetic genius, *Biographia Literaria* 2: 14–15.

Notes to Chapter 6

See also my *Imagery of Keats and Shelley* (Chapel Hill, 1949), pp. 264–266. Critical controversy on the *Ode to the West Wind* was vigorously fomented by F. R. Leavis in his *Revaluation* (1936). His extremely unfavorable view of the poem was shared by various American new critics. The question of its value was reopened in 1971 by Roy Fuller's lecture, printed in the *Times Literary Supplement* (May 14), which called forth Leavis's counterattack a week later. A vigorous correspondence then continued in subsequent issues through June 14, in which Desmond King-Hele and a number of others joined.

Notes to Chapter 7

1. *Coleridge's Shakespearean Criticism,* ed. T. M. Raysor (Cambridge, Mass., 1930), 1:196. See also pp. 126—131. 2. Ibid., p. 198. 3. *History of Aesthetic,* 2nd ed. (London, 1949), p. 187. (First printed in 1904.) 4. " . . . Let not the advocates of injustice and superstition flatter themselves that I should take Aeschylus rather than Plato as my model" (Preface). 5. See also the following lines. 6. "He [Shelley] seldom takes a gross, palpable, near-at-hand object from the world of ordinary perception and holds it for contemplation: his eye goes up to the sky, he starts with objects that are just on the verge of becoming invisible or inaudible or intangible and he strains away even from these." (Frederick A. Pottle, "The Case of Shelley," *PMLA* 67, 1952: 589—608.)

L. J. Zillman gives an elaborate account of critiques of *Prometheus Unbound* in his 1959 variorum edition of the poem (Seattle, Wash.). In recent years there have been many careful readings. Milton Wilson provides one of the most central of these in *Shelley's Later Poetry* (New York, 1959); in the same year Harold Bloom in *Shelley's Mythmaking* (New Haven) introduced for the first time the outlook of modern mythicism in his approach. More recently E. R. Wasserman has systematically restudied *Prometheus Unbound* in a volume of 1965 and his *Shelley: A Critical Reading* (1971)—both works from the Johns Hopkins Press. My own outlook on *Prometheus* still stresses the crucial Shelleyan tension between "image and imagelessness." Lloyd Robert Abbey has furnished a keen and challenging interpretation in an unpublished 1971 University of Toronto dissertation devoted to the central configuration of Shelley's imagery and metaphor.

Notes to Chapter 8

1. *The Divine Comedy,* trans. Thomas Bergin (New York, 1955).

Taaffe's 1822 commentary is reproduced in my "John Taaffe's Annotated Copy of *Adonais*," *Keats-Shelley Journal* 17 (1968): 31–52. I owe my reference to "progressive revelation" to Wasserman, *The Subtler Language* (Baltimore, 1959). Glenn O'Malley in *Shelley and Synesthesia* (Evanston, 1964) has thoroughly analyzed the star-flower pattern in *Adonais*.

Notes to Chapter 9

1. *Modern Poetry and the Tradition* (Chapel Hill, N.C., 1939), p. 31. 2. "A Reading of Keats," *On the Limits of Poetry* (New York, 1948), p. 177. 3. *Mythology and the Romantic Tradition in English Poetry* (Cambridge, Mass., 1937), p. 107. 4. Introduction, *Poems of John Keats*, ed. G. Thorn Drury (New York, n.d.), p. lxiv. 5. *Keats* (Oxford, 1926), pp. 113–114. 6. See Sidney Colvin, "A Morning's Walk in a Hampstead Garden," in *The John Keats Memorial Volume* (London, 1921), p. 73. 7. Hyder E. Rollins, ed., *The Letters of John Keats, 1814–1821*, 2 vols. (Cambridge, Mass., 1958), 1: 184. Punctuation and capital letters altered. 8. "Aesthetic Pattern in Keats's Odes," *University of Toronto Quarterly* 12 (1943): 167–168. 9. *The Letters of John Keats*, 1: 192. 10. "Longinus," in *Lecturers in Criticism*, ed. Elliott Coleman (New York, 1949), pp. 61–62. 11. *Revaluation* (London, 1936), p. 244. 12. *The Letters of John Keats*, 1: 238–239. 13. *Keats*, p. 111. 14. "Prometheus and the Aeolian Lyre," *Yale Review* 33 (1944): 495.

There have been many good readings of the *Ode to a Nightingale* since this essay was written, but they have been chiefly devoted to its relation to the other "great odes" of Keats, and ordinarily to placing the poem in the development of Keats's thought. In my own work I should wish to emphasize the "romantic wit" of the poem and the concept of multiple, flexible planes in it and the other odes.

Notes to Chapter 10

1. I refer to *Keats and Shakespeare, A Study of Keats' Poetic Life from 1816 to 1820* (London, 1925), and *Keats*, 4th ed. (New York, 1955). First edition entitled *Studies in Keats* (1930). 2. See *Keats and Shakespeare*, pp. 28ff.; *Keats*, pp. 227–237. 3. E.g., *Keats*, pp. 259, 261. 4. *Keats*, p. 232. 5. *Keats*, pp. 252, 253.

Notes to Chapter 11

1. *Practical Criticism* (London, 1929), pp. 182, 207. 2. *Hawthorne* (New York, 1879), pp. 57–59. 3. "The Genius of Nathaniel Hawthorne," *North American Review* 274 (September 1879). *Herman Melville: Representative Selections*, ed. Willard Thorp (New York, 1938), pp. 332–333. 5. Ibid., p. 342. 6. James, *Hawthorne*, p. 54. 7. Cf. my comments on this passage in *Hawthorne's Fiction*, rev. ed. (Norman, Okla., 1964), pp. 31–32. 8. Cf. ibid., pp. 111–112.

Notes to Chapter 12

1. References are to canto and line numbers of the Constable edition of *Clarel.*

Notes to Chapter 13

On *Clarel* Walter E. Bezanson's edition (New York, 1960) stands alone, both for text and commentary. It will undoubtedly be fully utilized in the currently appearing Northwestern-Newberry Library edition of Melville's works. I draw here from the older Constable Standard edition, which is somewhat differently arranged as to formal divisions.

Notes to Chapter 14

Robert Penn Warren's "Melville the Poet," published in the *Kenyon Review* 8 (Spring 1946), and greatly extended in "Melville's Poems," *Southern Review*, n.s. 3 (1967): 799–855, is a classic study. Newton Arvin provided sensitive comment in his 1950 American Men of Letters series *Herman Melville* (New York).

Notes to Chapter 15

W. T. Stafford, ed., *Melville's Billy Budd and the Critics* (San Francisco, 1961) is representative of critical approaches, and H. Hayford and Merton Sealts present an annotated list of interpretations in their careful edition, *Billy Budd, Sailor* (Chicago, 1962). Melville's tales have been a mirror for every man's opinions. I maintain my own stand (*Melville's Shorter Tales*, Norman, Okla., 1960) on their essential ambiguity and the special kind of irony present in them. More recently they have become a vehicle for activism, as in Kingsley Widmer's *The Ways of Nihilism* (The California State Colleges, 1970).

Index

Aeschylus, 71
Aristotle, 7, 14, 50, 71, 192, 193
Arnold, Matthew: *Empedocles on Etna*, 156, 166
Auden, W. H., 106

Babbitt, Irving, 93, 113
Barbauld, Anna Letitia, 32
Barnard, Ellsworth, 94
Bede, 48
Beerbohm, Max, 36, 116
Bell, Millicent: *Hawthorne's View of the Artist*, 11
Béranger, P. J. de, 166
Bergin, Thomas, 89
Blake, William: and Shelley, 75; the world of Urizen, 77; 103, 150, 194–
    195, 198
Bosanquet, Bernard: *A History of Aesthetic*, 71
Bradley, A. C., 117
Brahma, 67
Brawne, Fanny, 104, 119
Bridges, Robert, 108
Brooks, Cleanth, 60, 61, 100, 102, 108, 111
Brown, Stuart G., 100

Browning, Elizabeth Barrett, 166
Bryant, William Cullen, 166
Bush, Douglas, 100, 104
Byron, George Gordon, Lord, 3–4, 5, 6, 51, 165, 166

Coleridge, Samuel Taylor, 1, 5, 8, 12, 13–14, 17–59, 61; on romantic
    drama, 69–72; 75, 101, 106, 113, 114–115, 120, 121, 130, 150
    Biographia Literaria, 13–14, 20, 108, 150
    Christabel, 31, 186
    Dejection: An Ode, 17–18, 40, 53–59, 142–143
    The Aolian Harp, 17, 21, 23–25, 26
    Fears in Solitude, 17, 18
    Frost at Midnight, 17, 20, 21, 25–26
    Kubla Khan, 30, 31, 43–52, 95, 100, 102, 108
    The Nightingale, 17, 18
    Reflections on Having Left a Place of Retirement, 17, 18–19
    The Rime of the Ancient Mariner, 27–42, 74–75
    This Lime-Tree Bower My Prison, 12, 17, 19, 20, 21, 22, 23
    To William Wordsworth, 17
Colvin, Sidney, 100, 117
Croce, Benedetto, 75

Dante Alighieri: *Paradiso*, 87–97, 99; order and degree in, 92
De Sélincourt, Ernest, 54, 100
Dickinson, Emily, 181
Douglas, Norman: *South Wind*, 166
Dunbar, William: *Lament for the Makaris*, 143

Eliot, T. S.: 15–16, 61, 111; *Idea of a Christian Society*, 181; *Notes towards
    the Definition of Culture*, 181
Emerson, Ralph Waldo, 9, 11, 150, 166

Fancy, 12–13
Fielding, Henry, 124
Frye, Northrop, 5, 7

Garrod, H. W., on *Ode to a Nightingale*, 100, 108, 113–114
Genre, Coleridge on, 19–20; romantic, 27–42, 69–72
Gittings, Robert, 119–120
Goethe, Johann Wolfgang von, 9, 75
Guérard, Albert, Jr., 100, 114

Harper, George MacLean, 17
Hawthorne, Julian, 4, 172

Hawthorne, Nathaniel: 1–16; romanticism in, 11–13; 108, 124–136, 166, 172–173
 The Blithedale Romance, 173
 Main-Street, 125
 The Marble Faun, 6, 172
 Mosses from an Old Manse, 125, 129
 My Kinsman, Major Molineux, 134–136
 The Scarlet Letter, 128, 131
 Twice-Told Tales: 1851 Preface, 124
 Young Goodman Brown, 128, 131, 132–134
Heine, Heinrich, 166
Heyerdahl, Thor, 159
Hierarchy: in *Ancient Mariner*, 38
Hood, Thomas, 166
Horace, 18, 21
Housman, A. E., 24
Howells, William Dean, 13
Hulme, T. E., 13, 179
Hutchinson, Sara, 54
Huxley, Aldous, 166

Illusion: Coleridge on, 28–33; in *Ode to a Nightingale*, 35
Imagination, 12–13, 27, 29–30, 32, 33, 35, 57–59, 69–70, 101–115

James, D. G.: *The Romantic Comedy*, 17–19
James, Henry: 8, 13, 124; on Hawthorne, 126–128, 129, 130, 131–132
James, Henry, Sr., 125
Jones, Mrs. Isabella, 119
Joy: in *Dejection: An Ode*, 57, 59

Kapstein, I. J., 63
Keats, John: 4, 5, 31, 49, 51, 98, 100–123, 186
 The Eve of St. Agnes, 31, 100, 119
 The Fall of Hyperion, 118–119
 Hyperion, 118–119
 King Otho, 118
 La Belle Dame Sans Merci, 34
 Lamia, 118
 Ode on Melancholy, 101, 103
 Ode to a Nightingale, 35, 43, 100–115, 119
 A Song of Opposites, 101
 To Autumn, 103, 113, 117
Keats, Thomas, 104
Knight, G. Wilson, 100

La Bruyère, Jean de, 166
Lamb, Charles, 19, 22
Leavis, F. R., 100, 112
Levin, David, 132
Leyda, Jay: *The Melville Log*, 23
Longinus, 15, 50, 89, 111–112
Lowell, Amy, 119
Lowes, John Livingston, 43, 44

McLuhan, Marshall: on *Ode to a Nightingale*, 100, 110, 114
Marvell, Andrew, 166; *Appleton House*, 196
Melville, Herman: 3, 4, 9, 10, 11, 38; review of Hawthorne's *Mosses*, 129–131; 137–209; hedonism in, 159–160
   The Admiral of the White, 139
   Bartleby, 177
   Battle-Pieces: 140, 141, 145, 146, 166, 182, 185, 187, 198; *The Conflict of Convictions*, 185; *Donelson*, 186; *Inscription*, 160; *Lee in the Capitol*, 145; *The March into Virginia*, 188; *A Meditation*, 145; *Misgivings*, 188; *On the House-Top*, 186, 198; *On the Slain Collegians*, 145; *The Scout toward Aldie*, 141; *A Utilitarian View of the Monitor's Flight*, 189
   Benito Cereno, 158, 197
   Billy Budd: 137, 141, 191–209; irony in, 191–192; as tragedy, 192–193
   Clarel, 137–140, 141, 145, 146, 148, 157, 159, 160, 162, 165–183, 198
   The Confidence-Man, 165
   Ditty of Aristippus, 187
   The Encantadas, 138, 139
   John Marr and Other Sailors: 140–149, 150, 186, 198; *The Aeolian Harp*, 146; *The Berg*, 146; *Bridegroom Dick*, 143, 144–146, 198; *Far Off-Shore*, 146; *The Haglets*, 139, 146–147, 208; *John Marr*, 141–144, 186, 187; *The Maldive Shark*, 148; *Old Counsel*, 146; *Tom Deadlight*, 146
   Journal of a Visit to Europe and the Levant, 140, 157–158, 159, 166, 168, 177
   Marquis de Grandvin, 159, 186, 187; *In the Hostelry*, 159; *Naples in the Time of Bomba*, 159
   Moby Dick: 139, 141, 147, 149, 171, 192, 197, 207
   The Paradise of Bachelors, 197
   Rip Van Winkle, 186
   Timoleon: 149–159, 198; *After the Pleasure Party*, 153–154, 186, 188; *The Age of the Antonines*, 156, 199; *The Apparition*, 156; *The Archipelago*, 158; *Art*, 149; *The Attic Landscape*, 149; *The Bench of Boors*, 155, 156, 188; *The Enthusiast*, 154, 155; *Fragments of a Lost Gnostic Poem*, 150, 151–152, 198–199; *The Garden of Metrodorus*, 152; *The Great Pyramid*, 156–157;

Greek Architecture, 149; *Greek Masonry*, 149; *In a Bye-Canal*, 188; *In a Garret*, 149; *In the Desert*, 156; *Lamia's Song*, 155, 156; *Lone Founts*, 154–155; *Magian Wine*, 152; *The Margrave's Birthnight*, 152–153; *Monody*, 189–190; *The Night-March*, 152; *Off Cape Colonna*, 158; *The Parthenon*, 149, 186; *Pausilippo*, 158; *Pebbles*, 147, 148, 150, 188; *The Ravaged Villa*, 152; *Syra*, 158–159; *Timoleon*, 150–151, 186; *The Weaver*, 149

To Daniel Shepherd, 186
To Ned, 186
Weeds and Wildings with a Rose or Two: 159–163; *The American Aloe*, 160; *The Avatar*, 160; *A Ground Vine*, 160; *Immolated*, 161, 162; *Pontoosuce*, 161, 162; *Rammon*, 161, 162; *The Rose Farmer*, 161; *The Vial of Attar*, 161; *A Wayside Weed*, 160; *When Forth the Shepherd Leads the Flock*, 160

White-Jacket, 144
Milton, John, 22, 49, 71, 91, 97, 133, 182, 186
Moore, Thomas, 166
Motley, John Lothrop, 173
Murry, John Middleton: 116–123; *Keats*, 119–120; *Keats and Shakespeare*, 117–123

Organicism: 8–9, 12, 14; in Melville, 149–150

Picturesque, the: romantic, 47, 106
Plato, 44, 49, 50, 71, 94, 99
Pleasure: in romantic poetry, 30–33, 44–50
Poe, Edgar Allan, 11
Pope, Alexander, 15, 44, 103

Ransom, John Crowe, 60, 93, 111
Reynolds, Joshua, 166
Robinson, Henry Crabb, 166
Richards, I. A., 7, 111, 126
Ridley, M. R., 43
Romanticism: 9–16, 109–110; English and American, 5–6, 9–13
Rubin, Louis D., Jr., 9
Rymer, Thomas, critique on *Othello*, 7

St. John of the Cross, 98
Sappho's Ode, 111–112
Schiller, Johann Christoph Friedrich von, 166
Schneider, Elisabeth: on *Kubla Khan*, 43, 49, 53
Shakespeare, William, 4, 69, 116, 117, 118, 120, 121, 122

Shelley, Percy Bysshe: 5, 12, 51, 60–99; Platonism, 71–74, 102–103, 108, 166, 182
 Adonais: and Dante, 87f; synesthesia in, 92–93
 Alastor, 66, 91
 A Defence of Poetry, 66
 Lines Written among the Euganean Hills, 65
 Ode to the West Wind, 68
 A Philosophical View of Reform, 64–65
 Prometheus Unbound: 66, 69–86; as romantic drama, 69–71; imagery, 76–85; veil image, 82–85; "narrowing" image, 85–86; 91, 182, 208
 The Revolt of Islam, 63
Siva, 67
Slote, Bernice, *Keats and the Dramatic Principle*, 117–118
Smith, Fred Manning, 53
Stewart, Randall, 3
Symbol, 12, 55, 75; in Melville, 169

Taaffe, John, 87, 99
Tate, Allen: 60; on *Ode to a Nightingale*, 100, 103–105, 111
Taylor, Jeremy, 166
Tennyson, Alfred, Lord, 166
Thelwale, John, 19–20, 22–23
Thomas, Wright, 100
Thomson, James, 166
Thoreau, Henry David, 9
Thorpe, Clarence D., 116
Tillyard, E. M. W., 39
Trollope, Anthony: on *The Scarlet Letter*, 128–129

Understanding, 12

Vishnu, 67

Ward, J. A.: *The Search for Form*, 8
Warren, Robert Penn: 100, 111; on Melville's poetry, 184–185
Wasserman, Earl R.: on "progressive revelation," 92
Wellek, René, "Perspectivism," 8
White, Newman Ivey, 63
Whitman, Walt, 9, 150
Wilde, Oscar: *The Ballad of Reading Gaol*, 34
Wimsatt, William K., Jr., 4–5

Wordsworth, William: 5, 12, 36, 47, 51, 53, 185, 193
   Lines Written . . . Above Tintern Abbey, 20, 47
   Ode on Intimations of Immortality, 20, 53, 95, 109, 110, 114
   The Prelude, 20
   The Recluse, 91

Yeats, William Butler, 61, 75, 162, 186